# A BIBLIOGRAPHY OF T
## NEIL M GUI...

AUP Titles of related interest

**LANDSCAPE AND LIGHT**    *(NEW)*
**Essays by Neil M Gunn**
*edited by Alistair McCleery*

**TEN MODERN SCOTTISH NOVELS**
*Isobel Murray and Bob Tait*

**A BLASPHEMER AND REFORMER**
**A Study of Lewis Grassic Gibbon**
*William K. Malcolm*

# A BIBLIOGRAPHY OF THE WORKS OF NEIL M GUNN

C J L Stokoe

Published in association with Aberdeen City Libraries by
ABERDEEN UNIVERSITY PRESS

First published 1987
Aberdeen University Press
A member of the Pergamon Group

**British Library Cataloguing in Publication Data**

Stokoe, C. J. L.
　A bibliography of the works of Neil M. Gunn.
　1. Gunn, Neil M.——Bibliography
　I. Title
　016.828′91209　　　Z8375.5/

　ISBN 0-08-035079-8

Printed in Great Britain
The University Press
Aberdeen

# CONTENTS

**To My Wife**

Without whose understanding and help this work would not have been possible.

# PREFACE

### 1  *Purpose*

I was first introduced to the work of Neil M Gunn by Club Leabhar (The Highland Book Club) who chose to republish "The Serpent" as their first offering. For this I owe them a debt of gratitude as I subsequently embarked on a systematic reading of all of Gunn's work which has given me great delight.

A bibliography by Dr W R Aitken of Neil M Gunn's published books appeared in "Neil M Gunn; The Man and the Writer"—Blackwood 1973, but this was the only guide to his work available. For my own continued pleasure I sought out newspaper articles, details of broadcast material and the wealth of short stories and submissions to magazines on both sides of the Atlantic.

Having derived so much pleasure from these works, I set about preparing this bibliography to enable serious students and devotees to follow the path I have taken with less effort.

### 2  *Scope*

I have aimed to include in this bibliography reference to all of Neil M Gunn's known works whether published or not, together with a section relating to broadcast work. In a work of this kind, there will inevitably be some omissions but it has been researched over many years and is in as complete a form as I can achieve.

### 3  *Special Features*

The work has been grouped in six sections with an index. The sections cover short stories and books, plays and dramatisations, verse, articles in newspapers and periodicals, broadcast material and a miscellaneous section. Each section has been listed in chronological order and the first section has deliberately included both short stories and books so as to underline the extent to which his early material was re-used and his ideas developed. To further assist students, the entries in the first two sections, being the principal artistic output, and occasionally elsewhere have notes appended giving a brief, non-critical summary of the content. Apart from the index, a cross-referencing system has been produced.

In all cases, I have shown the title, publisher (or name of publication), place of publication, volume and issue number where applicable and date of publication.

In addition, for the published books, I have given full bibliographical information inclusive of a collation accounting for all leaves. In the section relating to broadcast material, the information given is; the title, date, description of the type of work, the producer, radio programme and duration. I have also tried to indicate where known, whether a script or recording exists.

### 4   *Research Methods and Acknowledgements*

Most of the research work has been carried out personally and I am indebted to many people and institutions. I have received great assistance from many libraries throughout the UK and in particular The National Library of Scotland in Edinburgh, The British Library in London and the The Bodleian Library in Oxford. It is always invidious to single out individuals but I must go on record in acknowledging my gratitude to the Executors of the late Neil M Gunn for allowing me access to his private papers at the National Library of Scotland, to Mr S M Simpson, Assistant Keeper of Manuscripts at the National Library of Scotland for his unfailing help and guidance, to Miss Elizabeth Sutter of the BBC in Glasgow for the tremendous help she afforded in preparing the section on broadcast material and to Professor Arnold Goldman for his guidance and encouragement throughout. Help with material for the bibliography came from Professor F R Hart, Dr W R Aitken, J B Pick and many others too numerous too mention. My thanks to all.

My research in the later stages was assisted by a grant from the British Academy which is acknowledged with thanks and with this financial support, research was carried out in the United States most ably by Mrs Patricia A R Thomas.

# CHRONOLOGY

1891      Neil Gunn born in Dunbeath
1907–11  Working in London and Edinburgh
1911      Begins his career in the Customs and Excise Service
1921      Marries Daisy Frew
1923      Begins career as writer, publishing short stories and articles
1924      Meets C M Grieve, 'Hugh MacDiarmid'
1926      *The Grey Coast*
1927      J B Salmond becomes editor of the *Scots Magazine*
1929      *Hidden Doors* (short stories). Joins Nationalist Party
1931      *Morning Tide* is a Book Society choice. Involvement in General Election
           on behalf of John MacCormick, Nationalist candidate for
           Inverness-shire
1932      *The Lost Glen*. Beginnings of estrangement from Grieve
1933      *Sun Circle*
1934      *Butcher's Broom*
1935      *Whisky and Scotland*
1937      *Highland River* published and wins James Tait Black Memorial Prize
           Neil Gunn resigns from the Customs and Excise Service to become a
           full-time writer. He sets off on the cruise from Skye to Inverness,
           through the Caledonian Canal, described in *Off in a Boat* (1938)
1938      Visit to Munich
1939      *Wild Geese Overhead*, a Book Society Choice
1940      *Second Sight*
1941      *The Silver Darlings*
1942      *Young Art and Old Hector*
1943      *The Serpent*
1944      *The Green Isle of the Great Deep*
1946      *The Key of the Chest*
1947      *The Drinking Well*
1948      *The Shadow, The Silver Bough*
1949      *The Lost Chart, Highland Pack* (essays)
1950      *The White Hour* (short stories)
1951      *The Well at the World's End*. Appointed to Commission of Inquiry into
           Crofting Conditions (Taylor Commission)
1952      *Bloodhunt*
1954      *The Other Landscape*
1956      *The Atom of Delight*

1963        Death of Daisy
1973        Death of Neil Gunn

The authoritative biography of Neil Gunn is *Neil M Gunn: A Highland Life* by F R Hart and J B Pick (Murray, London: 1981).

*A Bibliography of the Works of Neil M Gunn* by C J L Stokoe will be published by Aberdeen University Press in 1987.

**A**

BOOKS AND SHORT STORIES

A1                      (F1)

## THE APPLE TREE | THE APPLE TREE | LONDON

VOL 1   NO 2   PP 3 - 7            JUNE 1918

Prize winning short story in a competition announced in Vol 1 No 1 - May 1918 with a set title the same as that of the magazine.

This was the first short story of GUNN's to be published.

GUNN used the tree, laden with blossom, as a focal point for a romantic encounter recalled by a young man on his homeward train journey. He feels impelled to return and the tree again becomes a focal point. However, in the cold light of dawn, reality is poignantly different from the recollection.


A2                      (A5)

## THE SPECTRE OF THE SIGN-POST | PAN | LONDON

VOL 9   NO 23   PP 117 - 124        MAY 1923

Written under the Pseudonym of NEIL McPHEE

"Pan" Magazine was the predecessor of "20 Story Magazine".

Light-hearted story of mystery and romance introducing us to Mr. Lionel Jenkins, an author of mystery stories who we meet again in a later story. This is the first of GUNN's commercially accepted stories.

A3                    (A42)

VISIONING | THE SCOTTISH NATION | MONTROSE

VOL 1   NO 12   PP 4 - 5              24TH JULY 1923

This Story later appeared in:-

HIDDEN DOORS | PORPOISE PRESS | JULY 1930 | PP 23 - 37

A young armchair traveller knows many foreign places
intimately through regular discussions and story
telling sessions with sea-faring friends. However,
as a result of a chance liason he has a vision of
personal stagnation and exchanges a passive for an
active role in travelling.


A4                  (A15, A50, A110)

SURFACES | THE SCOTTISH NATION | MONTROSE

VOL 1   NO 14   PP 4 - 5              7TH AUGUST 1923

A story of romance between two young people, which
concentrates on intellectual qualities and inner
realities. In many ways this foreshadows the more
philosophical approach of his later novels. One
character is the daughter of an archaeologist, a
calling which appears often in GUNN's work.


A5          (A2, A14, A16, A27, A30, A95)

THE HOUSE ON THE MOOR | 20 STORY MAGAZINE | LONDON

VOL 3   NO 14   PP 121 - 125           AUGUST 1923

Written under the Pseudonym of NEIL McPHEE

A motorist on a moorland road discovers a lost
child, returns it to its impoverished but clean and
tidy home where it is ultimately re-united with its
parents. In the interim, fearing foul play, the

hero, a writer of detective fiction - see The Spectre Of The Sign Post - makes a discovery which will be to the benefit of all. This story has many pointers to later work; there is a personification of the moor as in much of his work - in particular the short story "Symbolical". The furniture in the house is also regarded as watching the hero as in "The White Hour". In the disposition of the buildings of the croft, the identity of the recently deceased grandfather and the final discovery this is clearly the forerunner of "The Grey Coast".

A6          (A22, A30, A42, A83, A98, A115)
    DOWN TO THE SEA | THE SCOTTISH NATION | MONTROSE
VOL 1  NO 18  PP 14 - 15          4TH SEPTEMBER 1923
This story later appeared in:-
HIDDEN DOORS | PORPOISE PRESS | JULY 1930 | PP 104-115
THE WHITE HOUR | FABER&FABER | 2ND OCT.1950 | PP214-221
A story of an old man who has lived by the sea all his life who makes a final journey "Down To The Sea" where he recalls scenes from his earlier life before accidentally drowning. The theme is similar to "Symbolical", "Such Stuff As Dreams", "Henry Drake Goes Home" and, in a way, "The Serpent".

A7
    THE HAT BOX | THE GLASGOW HERALD | GLASGOW
P4                          13TH OCTOBER 1923
Despite the title, this early story is in the nature of a fisherman's reminiscence.

4

The Story appears over the initials N.M.G.


A8                    (A42, A115)

THE CLOCK | THE SCOTTISH NATION | MONTROSE

VOL 1   NO 24   PP 6 - 7              16TH OCTOBER 1923

This story later appeared in:-

HIDDEN DOORS | PORPOISE PRESS | JULY 1930 | PP 92-103

THE WHITE HOUR | FABER&FABER | 2ND OCT.1950 | PP 117-184

The clock of the title is almost personified in this
story.   It was a wedding present from an ex-employer
to a woman whose husband had just saved him from
drowning.   The gift arrived at the time her husband
died following pneumonia contracted in the rescue.
The clock became the embodiment of evil and its
destruction was attended by more tragedy.


A9

A TIGHT CORNER | THE GLASGOW HERALD | GLASGOW

P4                              20TH OCTOBER 1923

The story concerns a narrow escape from capture
after a salmon poaching expedition.   There are many
similarities between this story and the many
semi-autobiographical references throughout GUNN's
work.   The story appears over the initials N.M.G.


A10

TALKING ABOUT SNAKES

A letter dated 1.11.1923 to NEIL M. GUNN from Odhams
Press encloses payment for a short story of the
above title.   No manuscript survives and I have been

5

unable to trace publication in any of the likely publications of the period produced by Odhams.

A11

THE GRAMOPHONE | THE SCOTTISH NATION | MONTROSE

VOL 2   NO 2   PP 8 - 9                    13TH NOVEMBER 1923

A young adolescent's growing awareness of things adult is sympathetically told in this story. This is shown through the medium of music from a gramophone (then a new toy) owned by an adult for whom the youth has great admiration.

A12

THE HIND | THE SCOTTISH NATION | MONTROSE

VOL 2   NO 6   PP 4 - 5                    11TH DECEMBER 1923

A light hearted tale of poaching and roguery which explains why one person acquired the odd nick-name of "The Hind".

Typescript held at the National Library of Scotland.

A13

THE WHITE PACKET

A letter dated 17.3.1924 to NEIL M. GUNN from Cassell and Co. encloses payment for a short story of the above title. No manuscript survives and I have been unable to trace publication in any of the likely publications of the period produced by Cassell.

A14          (A5, A42, A95, A101, A115)

THE WHITE HOUR | THE DUBLIN MAGAZINE | DUBLIN

VOL 1   NO 8   PP 741 - 744                    MARCH 1924

This story later appeared in:-

HIDDEN DOORS | PORPOISE PRESS | JULY 1930 | PP 133-141

STORM AND PRECIPICE | FABER & FABER | 1ST OCT.1942 |

PP 147 - 152

THE WHITE HOUR | FABER & FABER | 2ND OCT.1950 |

PP 80 - 85

The story of an old lady sensing imminent death who,
as a final act, encourages the match between her
granddaughter and a visiting young man.  In doing so
she recollects the first meaningful meeting between
her husband and herself.  A scene that was to be
recreated between the young people in a Phoenix like
manner.


A15              (A4, A42, A50, A110)

THE SLEEPING BINS | THE CORNHILL | LONDON

VOL 56  New Series  NO. 336  (No. 774)

PP 663 - 679                              JUNE 1924

This story later appeared in:-

HIDDEN DOORS | PORPOISE PRESS | JULY 1930 | PP 191-221

A light somewhat contrived, story of mystery,
romance, and wine, incorporating as one of its
principals, an archaeologist, a profession which
occurs a number of times in GUNN's work.


A16              (A5, A23, A26)

FURNITURE OF THE HEART | 20 STORY MAGAZINE | LONDON

VOL 4  NO 24  PP 55 - 60                    JUNE 1924

Written under the pseudonym of NEIL McPHEE.

A wealthy bachelor, interested in antiques and in particular in picking up a bargain, - as in "A Romance Of The Reel" - finds a lost child at the side of the road. In this there are similarities to "The House On The Moor". He takes on the duties of a parent with a resultant warming of his personality. There are many parallels with the story "Birdsong At Evening".


A17                    (A42)

THE UNCASHED CHEQUE | THE NORTHERN REVIEW | EDINBURGH

VOL 1  NO 2  PP 104 - 109              JUNE-JULY 1924

This story later appeared in:-

HIDDEN DOORS | PORPOISE PRESS | JULY 1930 | PP 116-132

A macabre and somewhat contrived tale of failure, poverty, despair and death in the face of potential relief, told as a story in a Gentlemens Club.


A18

AN ADVENTURE IN JEALOUSY | NORTHERN REVIEW | EDINBURGH

VOL 1  NO 3  PP 162 - 169              AUGUST 1924

An essentially realistic engineer is scathing of the romantic element of novels whilst reading them avidly. His wife secretly yearns for a degree of such excitement in their relationship and with the help of an author friend, engineers an "Adventure in Jealousy".

BETWEEN HEADLANDS | THE NORTHERN REVIEW | EDINBURGH

VOL 1   NO 24   PP 246 - 247              SEPTEMBER 1924

This story later appeared in:-

HIDDEN DOORS | PORPOISE PRESS | JULY 1930 | PP 170-175

Set along the "Grey Coast" the story of an elderly
couple who were devoted to one another but a little
aloof from others.  Because of a crime in youth they
had been forced to flee but in old age they had felt
the need to return as close as they dared to the
land of their birth - a strong theme in GUNN's work.


A20

ENTHUSIASMS | 20 STORY MAGAZINE | LONDON

VOL 5   NO 28   PP 74 - 78                OCTOBER 1924

Written under the pseudonym of NEIL McPHEE.

A light story, written to a formula with a twist at
the end, of a man given to enthusiasms - some good
and some not so good.


A21

SHEIKING | 20 STORY MAGAZINE | LONDON

Vol 5   NO 29   PP 103 - 106              NOVEMBER 1924

Written under the pseudonym of NEIL McPHEE

A humourous story of two henpecked husbands and
their attempts to resolve their problems.


A22        (A6, A30, A42, A83, A98, A115)

SUCH STUFF AS DREAMS | THE DUBLIN MAGAZINE | DUBLIN

VOL 3   NO 1   PP 489 - 493               FEBRUARY 1925

This story later appeared in:-

HIDDEN DOORS | PORPOISE PRESS | JULY 1930 | PP 38-49

THE WHITE HOUR | FABER & FABER | 2 OCT.1950 | PP 185-191

The story of a dying Highland emigrant in Canada, who feels an overwhelming need to visit the surroundings of his youth. A desire which in his sickness is met.


A23          (A16, A40, A102, B2, B23)

A ROMANCE OF THE REEL | CHAMBERS'S JOURNAL | EDINBURGH

SEVENTH SERIES

VOL 15

Published in three parts:-

PART I      NO.768   PP 577 - 580      15th August 1925

PART II     NO.769   PP 603 - 606      22nd August 1925

PART III    NO.770   PP 620 - 621      29th August 1925

A well constructed story of an elderly antique shop owner and his salmon fishing holiday which ended in near disaster. There are comparisons and links drawn throughout with a painting in his shop. There are slight similarities in parts of this story to "The Poaching At Grianan" and "The Green Isle Of The Great Deep".


A24   (A28, A33, A34, A40, A42, A51, A107, A115,

B2, B5, B23)

HALF LIGHT | THE CORNHILL | LONDON

VOL 59   NEW SERIES NO 353 (NO 791) PP 607 - 620

NOVEMBER   1925

This story later appeared in:-

HIDDEN DOORS | PORPOISE PRESS | JULY 1930 | PP 50-75

SCOTTISH SHORT STORIES (AN ANTHOLOGY) | FABER & FABER | 1932 | PP 393 - 413

THE WHITE HOUR | FABER & FABER | 2 OCT.1950 | PP 257-273

A native of the Northern Coasts enters University and is successful. He is bitter and scathing about the dead grey coast and of "Celtic Twilights". He seems however strangely drawn and returns as if in answer to some call to his essential being. Gradually his surroundings assert themselves and he associates himself closer with the past and his heritage, to the point of seeing in his mind's eye the ghost of harbours past. He, still grudgingly, begins to associate himself with the "Celtic Twilight" poets whose work he describes as dream poetry, a glimmering half light, beckoning... In that same northern half light, which gives enriched coloration, he takes to swimming in the sea where he is ultimately drawn into its bosom, a return to the life and source of livelihood of his ancestors.

Whilst his hero in this story returns home as a schoolmaster, which is socially acceptable, the pull of the homeland is a recurring feature in GUNN's work, in particular in "The Lost Glen", "Back Home" and "The Drinking Well".

See also:-  "Poaching at Grianan"

"The Ancient Fire"

"Beyond the Cage".


A25 (A35, A42, A46, A60, A118, A121, E86, E94, E96)

THE SEA | THE GLASGOW HERALD | GLASGOW

P 4                                    19TH JUNE 1926

This story was to be adapted into a prize winning
story of the same name which appeared in the Scots
Magazine January 1929.   It was later to form the
basis of the first part of "Morning Tide".

A moving story of a storm at sea seen through the
eyes of a child.

The story appears over the initials N.M.G.


A26                    (A16, A123)

     BIRDSONG AT EVENING | THE CORNHILL | LONDON

VOL 61   NEW SERIES    NO 363 (NO 801)

PP 298 - 314                        SEPTEMBER 1926

A superb story of adaptation to retirement and to
the realities of nature.   The essential rightness of
the natural law as opposed to conventional moral
codes is clearly defined and previews in certain
respects ideas which were to find their full
flowering in "Bloodhunt".


A27                    (A5)

     THE GREY COAST | JONATHAN CAPE | LONDON | 1926

First edition:-

THE GREY COAST | by | NEIL M GUNN | [ORNAMENT] | [ital]
I ken a gloghole | That looks at the sky | As ·much  as
to say | "I'm as deep as you're high" | HUGH M'DIARMID |
[space] | JONATHAN CAPE LIMITED | THIRTY BEDFORD
SQUARE LONDON.

Collation: [A]$^8$, B - I$^8$, No J,K - U$^8$, 160 Leaves.

p. [1] THE GREY COAST; p. [2] blank; p. [3] TITLE
PAGE; p. [4] Publishers and printers notices; FIRST
PUBLISHED IN MCMXXVI: p. [5] to | MY MOTHER; p. [6]
blank; p. 7 - 320 text.

5" x 7 13/16". BOUND IN BLUE CLOTH: Spine stamped
in gold:

THREE HORIZONTAL LINES | THE | GREY | COAST | [ORNAMENT] |
NEIL M GUNN | [SPACE] | JONATHAN CAPE | THREE
HORIZONTAL LINES | REAR BOARD HAS PUBLISHERS MOTIF
IMPRESSED.

The above text was published in the U.S.A. by
LITTLE, BROWN of Boston in 1926. It was also
reprinted by CEDRIC CHIVERS LTD, Bath, at the
request of the London and Home Counties Branch of
the Library Association [1965] and by SOUVENIR
PRESS, LONDON, in 1976.

The novel was re-issued in April 1931 by PORPOISE
PRESS following the success of Morning Tide and
copyright was transferred to them by CAPE. The
author carefully revised the text making alterations
on more than 160 of its pages. The changes were
mainly in the interest of simplicity, directness or
precision - see Dr Aitken's comments in | Neil M
Gunn: The Man and the Writer | Ed. A. Scott and
D. Gifford, | William Blackwood | Edinburgh | 1973 | .
This is the only novel displaying textual variations
and it is unfortunate that later re-prints followed
the earlier text.

For detailed list of textual variations between the
two editions see Dr W R Aitken's article in:-

THE BIBLIOTHECK - A Scottish journal of Bibliography
and Allied Topics. Vol 6 No 4 1972.

Details of the second edition are:-

THE GREY COAST | BY | NEIL M. GUNN | [LINE] | I ken a
gloghole | That looks at the sky | As much as to say |
"I'm as deep as you're high" | HUGH M'DIARMID |
[SPACE] | EDINBURGH | [LINE] | THE PORPOISE PRESS

Collation:- [A]$^8$, B - 1$^8$, No J, K - U$^8$, 160 Leaves

p. [1] THE GREY COAST; p. [2] by the same author; p.
[3] TITLE PAGE; p. [4] Printing history: Publishers
and printers notices; p. [5] TO MY MOTHER; p. [6]
blank; p. [7] - [319] text; p. [320] blank.

4$^7/_8$" x 7$^1/_2$". BOUND IN BROWN CLOTH; Spine stamped
in gold: THE | GREY COAST | NEIL M | GUNN | [SPACE] |
PORPOISE | PRESS.

This is GUNN's first novel; A somewhat bitter one of
survival on the crofting coast of his native
Caithness. The story which centres round an old
man, his niece and her suitors, highlights the
decline of the area following the contraction of the
fishing industry and contrasts old and new values of
the people.


A28            (A24, A42, A126, C10)

        MUSICAL DOORS | THE CORNHILL | LONDON

VOL 62   NEW SERIES   NO 369   (NO 807)

PP 351 - 358                              MARCH 1927

This story later appeared under the title HIDDEN
DOORS in:-

 HIDDEN DOORS | PORPOISE PRESS | JULY 1930 | PP 176-190

A tale of the supernatural on a psychological plane, with celtic overtones. The main character, an Englishman, finds psychological doors opening to him in association with certain specific pieces, or types of music. The wild wind from the moor is music enough to open such a door and calls him, siren like, to the moor and his death.

There are in the dialogue parts of the story, which take place in the "intense white light illuminating the Soul" brought about by the consumption of whisky without drunkeness, early glimmerings of the type of dialogue employed in his later work, notably "The Other Landscape". On the Celtic side there are references to Marjorie Kennedy Fraser and similarities to "Half Light". Ironic reference is also made to "The Island that likes to be Visited" - see "Mary Rose" by J.M. Barrie.

A29

STRATH RUINS | CHAMBERS'S JOURNAL | EDINBURGH
SEVENTH SERIES VOL 17   NO 875   PP 625 - 630
3RD SEPTEMBER 1927
A tale of salmon poaching in a pool on the banks of which, are ruined croft houses. In a surprisingly humane way the clearances which caused the ruins are being continued through the game laws.

A30      (A5, A6, A22, A42, A83, A95, A115)
SYMBOLICAL | THE SCOTS MAGAZINE | DUNDEE
VOL 8   NO 3   PP 193 - 197              DECEMBER 1927

This story later appeared in:-

HIDDEN DOORS | PORPOISE PRESS | JULY 1930 | PP 82 - 91

STORM AND PRECIPICE | FABER & FABER | 1ST OCT. 1942 |

PP 153 - 159

THE WHITE HOUR | FABER & FABER | 2ND OCT. 1950 |

PP 58 - 64

A moving short story of a crofter's life and death struggle to win agricultural land from the moor. Death is a subject GUNN often explores in his short stories.


A31             (A76, A115, B20, E8)

THE BLACK WOOLLEN GLOVES | THE SCOTS MAGAZINE | DUNDEE

VOL 8   NO 4   PP 261 - 268              JANUARY 1928

This story later appeared in:-

THE WHITE HOUR | FABER & FABER | 2ND OCT. 1950 |

PP 118 - 127

Was later dramatised for Radio 8.2.1944.

A light-hearted romantic story with a surprise ending.


A32             (A42, A95, A115)

      BLAEBERRIES | THE SCOTS MAGAZINE | DUNDEE

VOL 8   NO 5   PP 325 - 327              FEBRUARY 1928

This story later appeared in:-

HIDDEN DOORS | PORPOISE PRESS | JULY 1930 | PP 76-81

STORM AND PRECIPICE | FABER & FABER | 1ST OCT. 1942 |

PP 76 - 79

THE WHITE HOUR | FABER & FABER | 2ND OCT. 1950 |

PP 65 - 68

ARGOSY | LONDON | VOL 12 NO 2 PP 85 - 87 FEB. 1951

A Superbly constructed short romance set on the grey crofting coast of Caithness.


A33 (A24, A34, A51, A107, B5, E4, E11, E36, E58)

THE MAN WHO CAME BACK (STUDY FOR A ONE ACT PLAY) |

THE SCOTS MAGAZINE | DUNDEE

VOL 8 NO 6 PP 419 - 429 MARCH 1928

A prose study of a crofters son who finds the call of his home too great. He leaves his education and training and returns only to be regarded as a failure. The play referred to was to be "Back Home". The theme was to be further developed in "The Drinking Well". There are also some similarities in "Half-Light" and "The Lost Glen". A Fragment of typescript is held at The National Library of Scotland.


A34

(A24,A33,A51,A107,A119,B5,E4,E11,E24,E36,E58)

THE LOST GLEN | THE SCOTS MAGAZINE | DUNDEE

A Novel serialised in eight parts.

Part I     CHAP 1-3 VOL 9 NO 1 PP 1-24 April 1928

Part II    CHAP 4-6 VOL 9 NO 2 PP 90-108 May 1928

Part III   CHAP 6-8 VOL 9 NO 3 PP 192-216 June 1928

Part IV    CHAP 8-10 VOL 9 NO 4 PP 283-308 July 1928

Part V     CHAP 11-13 VOL 9 NO 5 PP 360-384 Aug 1928

Part VI    CHAP 13-14 VOL 9 NO 6 PP 455-476 Sept 1928

Part VII   CHAP 15 VOL 10 NO 1 PP 63-80 Oct 1928

Part VIII CHAP 16 VOL 10 NO 2 PP 146-160 Nov 1928

Appeared in a slightly extended version as a published novel of the same title.

THE LOST GLEN | THE PORPOISE PRESS | 3.3.1932
A bitter novel set in the contemporary realities of a depopulated and dying Highland area. The hero has returned (as in "Back Home") under something of a cloud and is confronted with a retired Colonel for whom he has to act as gillie which underlines the failure aspect. Inevitably the book ends in tragedy. There was a suggestion that this book be serialised or dramatised for Radio but in the event they did not take up their option preferring to present another of his works. GUNN at the time indicated his relief as he stated that he liked this one the least of his novels. This may to some extent be due to the fact that it was hawked round many publishers, unsuccessfully, between the time of its serialisation and its ultimate publication by the Porpoise Press in the wake of the highly successful "Morning Tide".

An extract from this book was printed under the title "The Ancient Land" in:-
"A BOOK OF SCOTLAND" ED. G.F. MAINE | COLLINS | LONDON & GLASGOW | NEW AND ENLARGED EDITION 1950 | PAGE 163
FROM CHAP. 1 OF SERIAL & CHAP. 1 OF PART 2 OF BOOK |
There is a slight variation between the Serial and the book in this piece. The extract follows the published book.

A35

(A25, A42, A46, A60, A118, A121, E86, E94, E96)

THE SEA | THE SCOTS MAGAZINE | DUNDEE

VOL 10   NO 4   PP 243 - 251                    JANUARY 1929

This story later appeared in:-

HIDDEN DOORS | PORPOISE PRESS | JULY 1930 | PP 7 - 22

SCOTTISH SHORT STORIES ED. T. & J.F. HENDRY | PENGUIN |
1943 | PP 68 - 78

A dramatic story of a storm at sea viewed through
the eyes of a child.  It was to be expanded into the
first part of Morning Tide.  Prof. F.R. Hart in his
"Brief Memoir" in | Neil  M  Gunn:  The  Man  and  the
Writer | Ed. A. Scott & D. Gifford. | Blackwood |
Edinburgh | 1973 | notes that this was a prize winning
story.   The prize was in fact one of £30 for the
best short story, presented by the Scots Magazine
(The Scots Observer "Jottings" 12.1.29).  Hart also
mentions an essay entitled "A Sea Storm" which GUNN
did at his Junior School and this story could well
have grown from that essay.   A similar dramatic
situation appears in the short story "The Storm".
This story was adapted for Radio in "This is my
Country" No. 1 "From the Sea" 31.5.1963.
A nineteen minute broadcast on the Scottish Home
Service (Schools).

A36

10 M.P.H. | S.M.T. MAGAZINE | EDINBURGH

VOL 2   NO 3   PP 33 - 37                     MARCH 1929

A light-hearted tale of an early motoring incident
with an unexpected twist at the end.

This was the first contribution to the S.M.T. (Scottish Motor Traction) Magazine.


A37                    (A42, A115)

THE MOOR | THE SCOTS MAGAZINE | DUNDEE

VOL 11   NO 1   PP 10 - 18                    APRIL 1929

This story later appeared in:-

HIDDEN DOORS | PORPOISE PRESS | JULY 1930 | PP 153-169

SCOTTISH SHORT STORIES (AN ANTHOLOGY) | FABER & FABER |

1932 | PP 414 - 427

SCOTTISH SHORT STORIES (AN ANTHOLOGY) |

FABER & FABER | 1942 | PP 309-332

THE WHITE HOUR | FABER & FABER | 2ND OCT. 1950 |

PP 274 - 285

A story of youth and romance inextricably linked to the background of the moor of the title.  As in so many of his stories a sense of people and landscape being part of one overall picture is very strong.

A German Translation by F. Wolcken appeared in "Die Neue Rundschau" Vol 49   Part I   PP 355 - 365 April 1938   Under the title "Urlandschaft".


A38                    (A77, A115)

THE MIRROR | THE SCOTS MAGAZINE | DUNDEE

VOL 11   NO 3   PP 180 - 186                    JUNE 1929

This story later appeared in:-

THE WHITE HOUR | FABER & FABER | 2ND OCT 1950 |'

PP 158 - 166

A writer, disillusioned with city life, leaves Glasgow for the Highlands where he hopes to re-discover lost values. He finds instead however limitations within himself which prevent him expressing himself creatively and he returns. There are similarities here to "Wild Geese Overhead".

A39

    THE SECRET OF THE WOOD | S.M.T. MAGAZINE | EDINBURGH

VOL 3  NO 1  PP 66 - 68           JULY 1929

A light, haunting story of chance encounter and murder with a dramatic and unexpected conclusion.

A40

  (A23,A24,A46,A68,A80,A94,A100,A107,A116,A117,A119,

    A127,B1,B2,B14,B23,B27,E2,E36,E41,E58,E80,E85)

THE POACHING AT GRIANAN | THE SCOTS MAGAZINE | DUNDEE

A novel serialised in nine parts.

(Grianan means "The Sunny Place")

| | | | | | |
|---|---|---|---|---|---|
| Part I | CHAPS 1-2 | VOL 11 NO 6 | PP418-434 | Sept | 1929 |
| Part II | CHAPS 3-4 | VOL 12 NO 1 | PP 25-44 | Oct | 1929 |
| Part III | CHAPS 5-6 | VOL 12 NO 2 | PP116-131 | Nov | 1929 |
| Part IV | CHAPS 7-8 | VOL 12 NO 3 | PP200-217 | Dec | 1929 |
| Part V | CHAP 9 | VOL 12 NO 4 | PP287-300 | Jan | 1930 |
| Part VI | CHAP 10 | VOL 12 NO 5 | PP379-393 | Feb | 1930 |
| Part VII | CHAP 10-12 | VOL 12 NO 6 | PP455-473 | March | 1930 |
| Part VIII | CHAP 13 | VOL 13 NO 1 | PP 61-73 | April | 1930 |
| Part IX | CHAP 14 | VOL 13 NO 2 | PP144-154 | May | 1930 |

A story of three men from differing walks of life who go on holiday to the Highlands. For each there is a need to go in search of some enigmatic, healing, quality.   There follows a stirring tale of adventure, poaching and romance, centred around the Laird of Grianan who, from economic necessity, has leased out his ancestral lands to wealthy Americans for the shooting.   He now lives with his daughter in the lodge.

This is a most interesting work in that it was never published in book form and yet it became a great "Source" book for his later works.

There are similarities with "A Romance of the Reel" and "The Hawks Feather" which pre-date it, the latter by only one month, and "The Ancient Fire" and "Beyond the Cage" are obviously based on this work with "Second Sight" having certain affinities with it as well.

There are salmon poaching scenes in the story which seem to share the same base material as those in "Highland River", "The Atom of Delight", "Primitives in the Pool", "The Boy and the Salmon", "The Drinking Well", and "Morning Tide".

The name of old Hector is first coined in this work as a general factotum or "Orra" man at the Lodge.

The work also seems to hold within it the seeds of the idea which was later to become "Highland River" when one character says "People should want to go up a river as to the rarer places, the source!"

A41

THE CANINE GAFF | S.M.T. MAGAZINE | EDINBURGH

VOL 4   NO 5   PP 34 - 37                              MAY 1930

A tale of salmon fishing and an unusual dog.

A42

HIDDEN DOORS | THE PORPOISE PRESS | EDINBURGH
The first edition bears the imprint 1929 but the
publishers advise that the work was not issued until
July 1930.

First Edition:-

HIDDEN DOORS | NEIL M. GUNN | [WAVY HORIZONTAL LINE] |
[SPACE] | [ORNAMENT] | [WAVY HORIZONTAL LINE] |
EDINBURGH 1929 | THE PORPOISE PRESS

Collation:- [A]$^8$, B-1$^8$, No J, K-O$^8$, 112 leaves.

p [1] HIDDEN DOORS | TO MY WIFE; p [2] Blank; p [3]
Title Page; p [4] FIRST PUBLISHED IN 1929 BY | THE
PORPOISE PRESS | 133A GEORGE STREET | EDINBURGH, C |
[SPACE] | with acknowledgments to the Editors of | THE
DUBLIN MAGAZINE | THE SCOTTISH NATION | THE   NORTHERN
REVIEW | THE SCOTS MAGAZINE | THE CORNHILL | [SPACE] |
PRINTED   IN   SCOTLAND   BY   THE   EDINBURGH   PRESS,
EDINBURGH ; p 5 Contents ; p [6] Blank; p 7 - 221
Text; p [222] Blank; p [223] Blank; p [224] Blank.
COLLECTION OF THE UNDERMENTIONED SHORT STORIES.

1] THE SEA     A25, A35

2] VISIONING     A3

3] SUCH STUFF AS DREAMS     A22   *

4] HALF-LIGHT     A24   *

5] BLAEBERRIES     A32   *I-

6] SYMBOLICAL     A30   *I-

7] THE CLOCK     A8

8] DOWN TO THE SEA     A6   *

9] THE UNCASHED CHEQUE    A17

10] THE WHITE HOUR    A14   *I-

11] GENTLEMEN

12] THE MOOR    A37   *

13] BETWEEN HEADLANDS    A19

14] HIDDEN DOORS    A28

15] THE SLEEPING BINS    A15

* Also appear in "THE WHITE HOUR - 1950   A115

I- Also appear in "STORM AND PRECIPICE" 1942   A95


5" x $7^1/_2$", BOUND IN ORANGE CLOTH; Spine stamped in
black: HIDDEN | DOORS | [LINE] | GUNN | [SPACE] |
PORPOISE; FRONT BOARD : HIDDEN DOORS | NEIL M. GUNN.
I have been unable to trace a previous publication of
the short story "Gentlemen".

A43                    (A98, C5, C9)

THE WILD | THE MODERN SCOT | DUNDEE

VOL 1   NO 2   PP 17 - 19                    SUMMER 1930
A complex, perhaps partially autobiographical, short
story.  The narrator is a recluse who recounts how,
from a vivid boyhood memory of time spent out of
doors, his affinity with the wild became impressed
upon him.  A poem came to be written epitomising this
experience which was recalled later during his urban
existence as an escape.  The need to escape became
increasingly strong leading eventually to his present
state.
Assuming    the    story    is    to    some    extent
autobiographical, the poem is likely to be either

"The Serpent" or, less likely, "O Sun" which fit the subject matter.

A44

PUPPETS | S.M.T. MAGAZINE | EDINBURGH

VOL 5  NO 3  PP 46 - 50                    SEPTEMBER 1930

The Narrator tells of a visit to an author friend to offer advice, as in the past, on an enmeshed plot. The author's problem with the plot is aggravated by being essentially autobiographical. A solution is offered which has far reaching results.

The idea, if not the result, may have been suggested by GUNN's reported assistance to Maurice Walsh who periodically experienced problems with his plots. (See Prof. Hart's Essay in | Neil M. Gunn : The man and the Writer | Blackwood | Edinburgh | 1973)

A45                        (A119)

SEA TANGLE | THE SCOTS MAGAZINE | DUNDEE

VOL 14  NO 3  PP 207 - 215                  DECEMBER 1930

A romantic fantasy of a young man who meets a green clad young maiden at the sea's edge who is perhaps a little more than human. A delightfully fresh story.

A46        (A25, A35, A40, A95, E51, E52)

MORNING TIDE | THE PORPOISE PRESS | EDINBURGH

Some copies of the first edition carry the date 1930. It is thought that publication was planned for late 1930 but was deferred, and the imprint date amended whilst in the press, following its being selected as

25

the book society choice for Jan. 1931.

First Edition:-

MORNING TIDE | by | NEIL M. GUNN | [LINE] | [SPACE] |
Edinburgh | [LINE] | THE PORPOISE PRESS.

Collation:- [A]$^8$, B-1$^8$, No J, K-S$^8$, 144 leaves p [1]
MORNING TIDE; p [2] by the same author; p [3] Title
Page; p [4] Publishers and Printers notices: FIRST
PUBLISHED IN MCMXXXI; p [5] TO JESS; p [6] Blank;
p 7 - 287 Text; p [288] Blank.

It seems likely that "Jess" of the dedication is his
wife, usually referred to as Daisy, who was born
Jessie Frew.

5" x 7$^5$/$_8$", BOUND IN GREEN CLOTH; Spine stamped in
gold: MORNING | TIDE | NEIL M. | GUNN | [SPACE] |
PORPOISE | PRESS

Later Editions:-

Edition illustrated by Maitland de Gogorza | HARCOURT
BRACE | NEW YORK | 1931

FABER & FABER | LONDON | 1932  The Faber Library, 7.

PENGUIN BOOKS | LONDON | 1936  Penguin Books 51.

TAUCHNITZ | BERLIN | 1938

FABER & FABER | LONDON 1953  New edition - reset.

SOUVENIR PRESS LTD | LONDON 1975

An extract entitled "Up from the Sea", comprising
chapter 1 of part one of the novel appeared in an
anthology "The Thistle and the Pen" edited by Eric
Linklater.  Published by Thomas Nelson and Sons Ltd,
London & Edinburgh, 1950.  PP 114 - 122

The same extract also appeared under the same title
in:-

26

| STORM AND PRECIPICE | FABER & FABER | LONDON |
1ST OCT. 1942 | PP 10 - 18
This is the novel which established GUNN's
reputation. It is a sensitive study of boyhood and
adolescence set in Gunn's native strath and with many
autogiographical overtones. In the first part the
short story "The Sea" is expanded into a highly
dramatic interlude.
His home at Inverness "Larachan" is reputed to have
been paid for with the royalties from the novel.
This book was to have been filmed by Associated
British Picture Corporation Ltd. A shooting script
was produced by Gilbert Gunn 3.1.1952 but the picture
does not seem to have been proceeded with.

A47

TRAGEDY INTO DREAM | THE MODERN SCOT | ST. ANDREWS
VOL 2   NO 1   PP 64 - 65                    SPRING 1931
A very short, complex story, almost a prose poem,
relating to an amour and incorporating an involved
dream sequence.

A48                         (A115)

PAPER BOATS | THE SCOTS MAGAZINE | DUNDEE
VOL 15   NO 1   PP 29 - 33                    APRIL 1931
This story later appeared in:-
THE WHITE HOUR | FABER & FABER | 2ND OCT 1950 | PP 51-57
A story, expressed as childs play, which makes a
serious observation of the conflict between man and
man, and man and the sea.

A49 (A105)

THE DEAD SEAMAN | THE SCOTS MAGAZINE | DUNDEE

VOL 15  NO 4  PP 265 - 289                    JULY 1931

A powerful story of two brothers, shepherds, living physically and metaphorically at the edge of a small crofting community, and of a dead seaman from a vessel wrecked in a storm.  The seaman had a bruised throat and may have been strangled;  was it accident or murder?

This story forms the basis of the novel "The Key of the Chest".


A50               (A4, A15, A110)

THE CIRCLE | THE SCOTS MAGAZINE | DUNDEE

VOL 16  NO 4  PP 241 - 255                  JANUARY 1932

A story of an archaeologist who is excavating a druidic circle with the assistance of an idiot.  As the work progresses the site exerts its own influence over the humans.

This story formed the basis of the novel "The Silver Bough".


A51 (A24, A33, A34, A107, A119, B5, E4, E11, E24)

THE LOST GLEN | THE PORPOISE PRESS | EDINBURGH

                                     3RD MARCH 1932

First Edition:-

THE LOST GLEN | by | NEIL M. GUNN | [LINE] | [SPACE] | EDINBURGH | [LINE] | THE PORPOISE PRESS

Collation:- [A]$^8$, B-1$^8$, No J, K-U$^8$, No V&W,X-Y$^8$ 176 leaves.

p [1] THE LOST GLEN; p [2] by the same author; p [3]
Title Page; p [4] Publishers and printers notices:
FIRST PUBLISHED IN 1932; p [5] TO MAURICE WALSH;
p [6] blank; p [7] PART ONE; p [8] Blank; p 9-351
Text; p [352] Blank.

5" x $7^5/_8$". BOUND IN BLUE CLOTH; Spine stamped in
gold: THE | LOST GLEN | NEIL M. | GUNN | [SPACE] |
PORPOISE | PRESS.

For details of this work see the entry dated April
1928 when this work first appeared as a serial.

Reprinted with a foreword by Dairmid Gunn by RICHARD DREW
PUBLISHERS | GLASGOW | 1985.

A letter from Faber & Faber to the Author 23.7.65
confirms that the copyright has reverted.

A52                    (A53, A95)

        THE OUTLINE | THE SCOTS MAGAZINE | DUNDEE

VOL 18  NO 6  PP 424 - 426              MARCH 1933

This story later appeared in:-

STORM AND PRECIPICE | FABER & FABER | 1ST OCT. 1942 |

PP 7 - 9

This piece which is an ariel view of Caithness and
the Northlands formed the introduction of:-

SUN CIRCLE | THE PORPOISE PRESS | 25TH MAY 1933 |

PP 7 - 10


A53                    (A52, A95)

        SUN CIRCLE | THE PORPOISE PRESS | EDINBURGH

                            25TH MAY 1933

First Edition:-

SUN CIRCLE | BY | NEIL M. GUNN | [LINE] | [SPACE] |

EDINBURGH | [LINE] | THE PORPOISE PRESS

<u>Collation</u>:- [A]$^8$,B-1$^8$,No.J,K-U$^8$, No.V&W, X-Z$^8$, 2A$^8$,

2B$^4$, 196 Leaves.

p [1] SUN CIRCLE; p [2] By the same author; p [3]

Title Page p [4] Publishers and printers notices:

FIRST PUBLISHED IN 1933; p [5] to J.B. SALMOND; p

[6] blank; p 7-391 Text; p [392] Blank

5" x 7$^5$/$_8$", BOUND IN RED CLOTH: Spine Stamped in

Gold: SUN | CIRCLE | NEIL M. | GUNN | [SPACE] | PORPOISE |

PRESS.

Reprinted by THE SOUVENIR PRESS | LONDON | 1983

The introduction of this novel "The Outline" was

published in:-

THE SCOTS MAGAZINE | DUNDEE | MARCH 1933 | PP 424-426

STORM AND PRECIPICE | FABER & FABER | 1ST OCT.1942 | PP

7 - 9

An historical novel set in Gunn's native Caithness at

the time of Norse raiding. It shows the interplay

between differing traditions, heritage and religions.


A letter from Faber & Faber to the Author confirms

that the copyright has reverted 23.7.1965.


A54                     (A115)

BRIDGE | SPECTATOR | LONDON

VOL 150   NO 5474   PP 755 - 6           26TH MAY 1933

This story later appeared in:-

THE WHITE HOUR | FABER & FABER | 2ND OCT. 1950 | PP28-32

AS "WHISTLE FOR BRIDGE".

A delicate story of a childs misconception. The

thrilling fantasy land of boyhood comes abruptly face

to face with adult reality.

A55                        (A115)

HILL FEVER | THE SCOTS MAGAZINE | DUNDEE

VOL 20   No 4   PP 264 - 268                    JANUARY 1934

This story later appeared in:-

THE WHITE HOUR | FABER & FABER | 2ND OCT.1950 | PP33-39

A young couple on Honeymoon in a remote fishing hut
in the midst of the Highlands: the husband begins to
feel a deep affinity with the landscape which is not
experienced to the same degree by his wife who feels
neglected.

A56                        (A132)

GEORGE AND THE DRAGON | THE SCOTS MAGAZINE | DUNDEE

VOL 21   NO 3   PP 188 - 207                    JUNE 1934

A journalist tracks down "Nessie" and manages to
photograph her. But through his preoccupation with a
scoop "Nessie" preserves her anonymity.

A57                        (A59, A95)

DARK MAIRI | THE SCOTS MAGAZINE | DUNDEE

VOL 21   NO 4   PP 264 - 274                    JULY 1934

This story later appeared in:-

STORM AND PRECIPICE | FABER & FABER | 1ST OCT. 1942 |

PP 126 - 139

This piece sets the scene and describes one of the
main characters in the novel "Butchers Broom" of
which it forms the first chapter.

BUTCHERS BROOM | THE PORPOISE PRESS | 1935 | PP 7 - 22

31

A58             (B7, B12, E3)

HIGHLAND HOSPITALITY | THE SCOTS MAGAZINE | DUNDEE

VOL 22  NO 3  PP 199 - 201             DECEMBER 1934

Typescript held at the National Library of Scotland.

The story recounts the initial aggression experienced

by a painter who wishes to draw a Highland Dwelling;

an aggression which later warms into the typical

Celtic welcome.

There are similarities to "Old Music" in the way a

welcome is expected.


A59             (A57,A95,B24,D198,E25,E101)

BUTCHER'S BROOM | THE PORPOISE PRESS | EDINBURGH

1934

First Edition:-

BUTCHER'S BROOM | BY | NEIL M. GUNN | [LINE] | [SPACE]

| EDINBURGH | [LINE] | THE PORPOISE PRESS

Collation:-[A]$^8$, B-1$^8$, No.J, K-U$^8$, No V&W, X-Z$^8$, 2A-

2D$^8$, 216 Leaves

p [1] BUTCHER'S BROOM; p [2] by the same author; p

[3] Title Page; p [4] Publishers and printers

notices: FIRST PUBLISHED IN 1934; p [5] to JOHN

GEORGE SUTHERLAND; p [6] ACKNOWLEDGEMENT THAT POEMS

USED ARE TAKEN FROM CARMINA GADELICA; p 7-429 Text; p

[430] blank; p [431] blank; p [432] blank.

5" x 7$^5$/$_8$", BOUND IN GREEN CLOTH; Spine stamped in

Gold: BUTCHER'S | BROOM | [ORNAMENT] | NEIL M. GUNN |

[SPACE] | PORPOISE | PRESS

Reprinted by:-

CEDRIC CHIVERS & CO. LTD. | BATH | 1965 (AT THE REQUEST OF THE LONDON AND HOME COUNTIES BRANCH OF THE LIBRARY ASSOCIATION)

SOUVENIR PRESS LTD. | LONDON | 1977

Other Editions:-

With title ; Exiles from their Father's Land.

Auswahl aus dem Roman Butcher's Broom.

Bearbeitet von W. Frerichs. Braunschweig: Westermann, 1939

With Title: Highland Night, illustrated by Freda Bone. New York: Harcourt, Brace, 1935

An extract entitled "Dark Mairi" comprising Chapter 1 of Part one of the novel appeared in:-

THE SCOTS MAGAZINE | DUNDEE | VOL 21 NO 4 | PP 264-274 | JULY 1934

STORM AND PRECIPICE | FABER & FABER | 1ST OCT. 1942 | PP 126 - 139

An extract entitled "The Swallow" comprising part of Page 31 of the novel appeared in:-

STORM AND PRECIPICE | FABER & FABER | 1ST OCT. 1942 | PAGE 38

An extract entitled "Singing Linnet" comprising part of Page 344 and Pages 345 - 351 of the novel appeared in:-

STORM AND PRECIPICE | FABER & FABER | 1ST OCT. 1942 | PP 140 - 146

According to Prof.F.R.Hart in | Neil M. Gunn : The Man and the Writer | Blackwood | Edinburgh | 1973 |

The character "Dark Mairi" is based on an old woman GUNN saw at a celidh in Inverness.

An historical story set in the Strath of Kildonan,
Sutherland in the period leading up to and including
the infamous Clearances. It gives a vivid portrayal
of the way of life which was destroyed and whilst the
deed is rightly condemned GUNN treats the whole
problem with objective reasonableness.

The Sutherland the Book was dedicated to was Neil
Gunn's Brother in Law - Police Chief at Invergordon.


A60     (A25,A35,A42,A46,A118,A121,E86,E94,E96)

THE STORM | THE SCOTS MAGAZINE | DUNDEE

VOL 22   NO 5   PP 349 - 357                FEBRUARY 1935

A brilliant short story of a proud old man's battle
against a storm in an open boat.  The battle is as
much against loss of face in the community, which is
closely involved in the drama, as it is against the
elements.

The story in a re-written form appeared later as
"Ride the Gale" and was incorporated in "The Well at
the Worlds End" as a dramatic highlight.


A61                      (A63)

UISGEBEATHA | THE SCOTS MAGAZINE | DUNDEE

VOL 23   NO 5   PP 327 - 333                 AUGUST 1935

A reconstruction of the discovery of whisky and its
effects written with wit and poetic licence which
became the introductory chapter of:-

WHISKY AND SCOTLAND | GEORGE ROUTLEDGE AND SONS LTD. |
LONDON | 1935

Subtitled "A Practical and Spiritual Survey" and

issued in the Voice of Scotland Series.

A62                              (B10, B13)

THE GOLDEN AGE | NEWS CHRONICLE | LONDON

Page 9                          12TH OCTOBER 1935

A contrast is drawn here between our material golden age and that Elysian state which is thought to have once existed.  The story concerns a visit to the bank manager (a solid, fair but essentially soulless man – as in "Net Results") for investment in speculative shares.  He is told by the banker of a moving experience he had had on an evening fishing expedition.  They had met and entertained an old crofter in his 70's who was a Gaelic poet and "Full of Lore".  This man represented the previous golden age and had left an indelible impression on the banker, and, through him, the narrator.


A63

 (A61,B25,B31,B32,D88,D210,D218,D225,D236,D247,D258,
                    E24,E26)

WHISKY AND SCOTLAND | GEORGE ROUTLEDGE AND SONS LTD. |
LONDON                                        1935

First Edition:-

WHISKY & SCOTLAND | [ital] A Pratical and Spiritual Survey | by | NEIL M. GUNN | [Ornament] |
GEORGE ROUTLEDGE | AND SONS, LTD.  Broadway | House, Carter Lane, London, E.C. | 1935
Collation:-[ ]$^4$, A-I$^8$, No J, K-M$^8$, N$^4$, 104 leaves.
p [i] WHISKY AND SCOTLAND; p [ii] THE VOICE OF |

SCOTLAND | List of Titles; p [iii] Title Page; p [iv]
Publishers and printers notices: [ital] First
published 1935; p v TO THOSE | OUTSIDE THE PALE; p
[vi] Blank; p vii Contents; p [viii] Blank; p [1]
PART ONE | IN THE BEGINNING; p [2] Blank; p 3-[198]
Text; p [199] Printers Notice; p [200] Blank.
$4^7/_8$" x $7^1/_2$", BOUND IN GREEN CLOTH; Spine Stamped in
Gold: [line] | WHISKY | AND | SCOTLAND | NEIL M. | GUNN
[Space] | ROUTLEDGE | [line]
Ornament impressed blind on bottom right hand corner
of the front board.
Reprinted with a foreword by MICHAEL GRIEVE (son of
HUGH MacDIARMID) by SOUVENIR PRESS LTD | LONDON | 1977
An extract entitled "Uisgebeatha" comprising the
First Chapter of the book appeared in:-
THE SCOTS MAGAZINE | DUNDEE | VOL 23 NO 5 | PP327-333 |
AUGUST 1935.
GUNN's Classic treatise on Scotch Whisky.


A64                          (Al15)
            THE TREE | THE SCOTS MAGAZINE | DUNDEE
VOL 24   NO 5   PP 352 - 364              FEBRUARY 1936
This story later appeared in:-
THE WHITE HOUR | FABER & FABER | 2ND OCT. 1950 |
PP 86 - 103
The tree had been a source of disagreement between
the Major and his wife who wished it felled to
lighten the house. The Major found it aesthetically
pleasing and resisted. Following the untimely death
of his wife the Major's life became without point and

he began to feel hemmed in by his surroundings. He felt a need to honour his wife's wish but could not bring himself to the deed. In a troubled night of storm his wife came to him in a dream bringing light and release. Daylight revealed that the storm had resolved also the physical argument.

A65                    (A97, B6, B8)

RAW MATERIAL | OUTLOOK | EDINBURGH

VOL 1  NO 1  PP 53 - 62                    APRIL 1936

One day in the life of Fred the narrator, who is an architect, a writer, a devotee of community drama and a Scottish Nationalist, during which he is seeking an idea for a short story.

Employs a similar device to "Choosing a Play" and "The Listeners Tale."

A66                    (A115)

MONTROSE RIDES BY | SCOTTISH FIELD | GLASGOW

NO 404  PP 25 - 28                    AUGUST 1936

This story later appeared in:-

THE WHITE HOUR | FABER & FABER | 2ND OCT. 1950 |

PP 231 - 241

Set in Inverness during the time of Charles I and highlights the plight of ordinary people during a military campaign. They bear the brunt whatever the outcome.

A67

THE POSTER | THE SCOTS MAGAZINE | DUNDEE

VOL 25   NO 5   PP 346 - 348                    AUGUST 1936

The poster was commissioned by a transport company as an advertisement.   Through the intervention of the director's daughter the contract is awarded to an intense bona fide artist who produced an evocative and powerful work symbolising the possibility of release from urban squalor via transport.   This caused initial shock but found ultimate favour. Running parallel to the business relationship is an emotional relationship between the artist and his benefactress.

A68          (A40, A95, A100, E80, E85, E100)

HIGHLAND RIVER | THE PORPOISE PRESS | EDINBURGH

APRIL   1937

First Edition:-

HIGHLAND RIVER | by | NEIL M. GUNN | [space] | Edinburgh | THE PORPOISE PRESS

Collation:-[A]$^8$, B-I$^8$, No J, K-U$^8$, No V & W, X-Y$^8$, 176 Leaves

p [1] Blank; p [2] Blank; p [3] HIGHLAND RIVER; p [4] by the same author; p [5] Title Page; p [6] [ital] Publishers and printers notices: First published in April MCMXXXVII; p [7] LETTER OF DEDICATION TO HIS BROTHER JOHN; p [8] Blank; p 9 - [348] Text; p [349]-[352] Blank.

5" x 7$^1$/$_2$".   BOUND IN TURQUOISE BLUE CLOTH: Spine stamped in Silver: Highland | River | Neil M. | Gunn | [Space] | Porpoise | Press.   Decoration in the form of a winding river blocked in blue runs down the full length of the spine.

This novel won the James Tait Black Memorial Prize for 1937 and was later dramatised for Radio by John Wilson and produced 12.3.1962.

<u>Later Editions</u>:-

LIPPINCOTT | PHILADELPHIA | 1937

TAUCHNITZ | BERLIN | 1937

FABER & FABER | LONDON | 1942 (New Edition Re-set)

FABER & FABER | LONDON | 1943  Q Series

ARROW BOOKS | LONDON | 1960  Grey Arrow Series

ARROW BOOKS | LONDON | 1974  New Binding

HUTCHINSON LIBRARY SERVICES LTD | LONDON | 1974

An extract entitled "The Salmon Fight" comprising Chapter One of the Novel appeared in:-

STORM AND PRECIPICE | FABER & FABER | 1ST OCT. 1942 | PP 21 - 37

The same piece entitled "Highland River" appeared in the ARGOSY MAGAZINE | LONDON | VOL 4  NO 7 | PP 13 - 24 | AUGUST 1943.

An extract entitled "In the Wood" comprising part of Pages 237-238 of the novel appeared in:-

STORM AND PRECIPICE | FABER & FABER | 1ST OCT. 1942 | PP 19 - 20

An extract entitled "The River" comprising part of Page 239, PP 240 - 243 and part of Page 244 of the Novel appeared in:-

STORM AND PRECIPICE | FABER & FABER | 1ST OCT. 1942 | PP 71 - 75

An extract entitled "To the Source" comprising part of Page 337 and Pages 338 - 348 of the Novel appeared in:-

STORM AND PRECIPICE | FABER & FABER | 1ST OCT. 1942 |
PP 102 - 110

An extract entitled "A Highland Community" appeared
in SCOTLAND, AN ANTHOLOGY | CADOGAN BOOKS | LONDON |
1984 | PP 97 - 98

According to F.R.  Hart in | Neil M.   Gunn  -  The  Man
and the Writer | Blackwood | Edinburgh | 1973 | The
Brother  who  was  temporarily  blinded  in  war  time
referred to in the novel was John to whom the book is
dedicated.   He also states that the pilgrimage to the
source actually happened.   It was indeed foreshadowed
in "Poaching at Grianan".

The  hero  sets  out  to  trace  the  source  of  his  local
river  to  which  he  has  returned  after  wanderings.    In
finding  the  source  he  also  finds  himself  through
remembered  scenes  from  his  life  and  the  magic  of  his
surroundings; set in GUNN's native Caithness.

A69                         (A84, E16)

        THE  BOAT | THE SCOTS MAGAZINE | DUNDEE
VOL 28 NO 3 PP 186 - 194               DECEMBER 1937
A   story  of  a  newly  "cleared"  community  trying  to
adapt  to  new  skills  to  survive  on  the  rocky  coastal
lands.    Some  of  the  younger  men  acquire  a  leaky  old
boat  to  try  their  hand  at  fishing  and  meet  unexpected
problems at the hands of the press gang.

This  story  was  subsequently  used  as  the  basis  of
the first chapter of:-

THE SILVER DARLINGS | FABER & FABER | 24TH APR. 1941.

WHISKY | UNPUBLISHED

FROM ADDRESS 1925 - 1937

Typescript held at the National Library of Scotland. This story conveys GUNN's distaste for city life and in particular the teeming and poverty stricken tenements.   This follows closely the visit to the slums in "Wild Geese Overhead" and again ends in a bar although without the father being met.   There are also similarities to the one act play "Glendaruel".


A71          (A95, D53, D54, D220, E34, E54)

OFF IN A BOAT | FABER & FABER | LONDON

5TH MAY, 1938

First Edition:-

OFF IN A BOAT | by | Neil M. Gunn | [space] |

FABER AND FABER LTD | 24 Russell Square | London

Collation:-[A]$^8$, B-I$^8$, No J, K-U$^8$, No V&W, X-Y$^8$ 176 Leaves.

p [1] - [2] Blank; p [3] OFF IN A BOAT; p [4] By the same author; p [5] Title Page; p [6] Publishers and printers notices: FIRST PUBLISHED IN MAY MCMXXXVIII; p [7] DEDICATION "FOR THE CREW"; p [8] Blank; p 9 Contents; p [10] Blank; p 11-12 Illustrations; p 13-348 Text; p [349]-[352] Blank.

$5^1/_8$" x $8^1/_8$"; BOUND IN ORANGE CLOTH, Spine stamped in Blue: [4 wavy lines - horizontal] | OFF IN | A | BOAT | [4 wavy lines - horizontal] | Neil Gunn | [space] | FABER AND FABER

An extract entitled "Our First Anchorage" comprising

part of page 79 and pages 80-85 of the book appeared
in:-

STORM AND PRECIPICE | FABER & FABER | 1ST OCT. 1942 |
PP 111 - 116.

An extract entitled "On Iona" comprising part of Page
205, Pages 206 - 214 and part of page 215 of the book
appeared in:-

STORM AND PRECIPICE | FABER & FABER | 1ST OCT. 1942 |
PP 117 - 125.

An extract entitled "Columba - A Twentieth Century
Portrait" comprising part of Page 211 and Pages
212 - 213 appeared in:-

SCOTLAND - An Anthology, ED. MAURICE LINDSAY | ROBERT
HALE | NOV 1974 | PP 150 - 151

An extract entitled "A Twentieth Century Portrait"
comprising part of Page 211 and Page 212 - 214
appeared in:-

AN IONA ANTHOLOGY | ED. F. MARIAN McNEILL | THE IONA
COMMUNITY | GLASGOW | 1947 | PP 38 - 41

An extract entitled "The Island of the Druids"
comprising part of page 207, pages 208 - 209 and part
of page 210 appeared in:-

AN IONA ANTHOLOGY | ED. F. MARIAN McNEILL | THE IONA
COMMUNITY | GLASGOW | 1947 | PP 61 - 63

An extract entitled "A Highland Novelist" comprising
part of Page 205, Page 206 and part of Page 207
apeared in:-

AN IONA ANTHOLOGY | ED. F. MARIAN McNEILL | THE IONA
COMMUNITY | GLASGOW | 1947 | PP 93 - 94

An extract entitled "St. Oran's Chapel and Queen

Margaret" comprising part of page 227 and part of page 228 appeared in:-

AN IONA ANTHOLOGY | ED. F. MARIAN McNEILL | THE IONA COMMUNITY | GLASGOW | 1947 | PP 110 - 111

An extract entitled "The Abbey Church" comprising part of Pages 215 - 216 appeared in:-

AN IONA ANTHOLOGY | ED. F. MARIAN McNEILL | THE IONA COMMUNITY | GLASGOW | 1947 | PAGE 111

An extract entitled "Clach Brath" comprising part of page 230 appeared in:-

AN IONA ANTHOLOGY | ED. F. MARIAN McNEILL | THE IONA COMMUNITY | GLASGOW | 1947 | PAGE 113

An extract entitled "Reilig Odhrain" comprising parts of Pages 228 and 229 appeared in:-

AN IONA ANTHOLOGY | ED. F. MARIAN McNEILL | THE IONA COMMUNITY | GLASGOW | 1947 | PAGE 120

An article entitled "The Torranan Rocks" which forms part of the book appeared in:-

THE SCOTS MAGAZINE | DUNDEE | JAN 1938 | PP 275-286

The Crew to whom the book is dedicated is his wife. The book is illustrated with photographs taken by GUNN and his wife. The manuscript was the only one to be handwritten; all the others being typed by his wife from notes. The manuscript is held at the National Library of Scotland.

This travelogue is the story of an extended holiday taken by GUNN and his wife in an old boat round the Western Isles. The holiday coincided with him giving up his Customs and Excise job to take up writing full time.

SNOW IN MARCH | THE SCOTS MAGAZINE | DUNDEE

VOL 29   NO 3   PP 191 - 199                    JUNE 1938

In this story a spinster in her middle years, living
on a farm which had been her brother's, hears the
sound of new born lambs in the night during a
snowstorm.   Impelled to some extent by her maternal
instinct she goes out into the field.   She meets the
shepherd in the field and together they attend a
birth where the mother dies.   The lamb is brought
indoors and a cup of tea is made.   They talk in an
intimate atmosphere and the woman entertains romantic
notions.   These are dispelled when she notes the
affection between the maid and the shepherd.
Thoughts of real motherhood finally die like the
sheep.

Shorn of the bulk of the romantic overtones, this
story was inserted into the novel "The Shadow" to
provide dramatic impact.


A73                      (A115, A128, A129)

THE OLD MAN | S.M.T. MAGAZINE | EDINBURGH

VOL 20   NO 6   PP 33 - 37                     JUNE 1938

This story later appeared in:-

THE WHITE HOUR | FABER & FABER | 2ND OCT. 1950 | PP40-50

THE PENGUIN BOOK OF SHORT STORIES.   Ed. J.F.HENDRY |

PENGUIN | 1970 | PP 85 - 93

Subtitled "A Tale of the Tinkers", The old man of the
title is the patriarch and compassionate lawgiver of

his tribe.

A74                 (A80, B14, B29, D212, E44)

      KING BRUDE | THE SCOTS MAGAZINE | DUNDEE

VOL 30   NO 5   PP 359 - 371            FEBRUARY 1939

The Story of the Stalking of "King Brude" the most

sought after stag on the hill.

Chapter 10 of "Second Sight".


A75                       (A115)

   DANCE OF THE ATOMS | THE SCOTS MAGAZINE | DUNDEE

VOL 31   NO 5   PP 347 - 357             AUGUST 1939

This story later appeared in:-

THE WHITE HOUR | FABER & FABER | 2ND OCT. 1950 |

PP 128 - 142

A story of childhood and an eight year old budding

scientist who tries an experiment with disastrous

consequences and receives a salutory lesson.


A76                 (A31, B20, E8)

   THE LADY'S HAND BAG | S.M.T. MAGAZINE | EDINBURGH

VOL 23   NO 2   PP 27 - 30               AUGUST 1939

A comedy of youth and unrequited love with a very

similar plot to "The Black Woollen Gloves".


A77                 (A38, A70, A95)

     WILD GEESE OVERHEAD | FABER & FABER | LONDON

                               5th OCTOBER 1939

First Edition:-

WILD GEESE | OVERHEAD | by | Neil M. Gunn | [Space] |

FABER AND FABER | 24 Russell Square | London

<u>Collation</u>:-[A]$^8$, B-1$^8$, No J, K-U$^8$, No V & W, X$^8$, Y$^4$, 172 Leaves

p [1]-[2] Blank; p [3] WILD GEESE OVERHEAD; p [4] by the same Author; p [5] Title Page; p [6] [ital] Publishers and Printers Notices: First Published in October MCMXXXIX; p [7] For | TOSHON WALSH | p [8] Blank; p 9-341 For Text; p [342]-[344] Blank

5" x 7$^9$/$_{16}$". BOUND IN RED CLOTH; Spine Stamped in Gold:WILD GEESE | OVERHEAD | [ornament] | Neil M. | Gunn | [Space] | FABER AND | FABER

An extract entitled "Streets" comprising part of Page 81 and Pages 82 - 107 and part of Page 108 appeared in:-

STORM AND PRECIPICE | FABER & FABER | 1ST OCT. 1942 | PP 80 - 101

The same episode forms the basis of the short story "Whisky".

This particular dramatic episode is based, according to Prof. F.R. Hart in | Neil M. Gunn: The Man and the Writer | Blackwood | Edinburgh | 1973 | on a visit to a birth in an Edinburgh slum with a medical student who shared his digs (Aged 17-19) and a similar visit with John MacNair Reid later in Glasgow.

A letter to the Author from Faber & Faber DD 23.7.65 confirms the copyright had reverted to him.

The first of GUNN's books to deal with city life, Wild Geese Overhead contains many brilliant descriptions of the slum quarter of Glasgow. At the

46

same time there is a sensitive love story told and in many ways I regard this as being one of his better works.

A78                          (A113)

REVIVAL MEETING | THE SCOTS MAGAZINE | DUNDEE

VOL 32   NO 4   PP 273 - 279                JANUARY 1940

Set in Lewis it concerns a revival meeting in a crofting community and the movement of psychic forces both religious and secular. It would seem that this was born out of personal experience as it bears close similarity to the chapter "In Lewis" in "Highland Pack" and some similarity to part of the chapter "Drink and Religion" in "The Silver Darlings".

This story was offered to the B.B.C. 3.9.40 but declined.

Typescript held at the National Library of Scotland.

A79

FREEDOM IS A NOBLE THING | S.M.T. MAGAZINE | EDINBURGH

VOL 25   NO 1   PP 26 - 29                JANUARY 1940

An interesting story of the rising under Wallace and Bruce through the eyes of an infantryman from Moray.

A80          (A40,A74,A117,B14,B29,D212,E44)

SECOND SIGHT | FABER & FABER | LONDON

11th APRIL 1940

First Edition:-

SECOND SIGHT | by | NEIL M. GUNN | [Space] |

FABER AND FABER | 24 Russell Square | London

<u>Collation</u>:- [A]$^8$, B-1$^8$, No J, K-U$^8$, No V & W, X$^4$, 164 Leaves.

p [1]-[2] Blank; p [3] SECOND SIGHT; p [4] by The Same Author; p [5] Title Page; p [6] [ital] Publishers and Printers Notices: First Published in April MCMXL; p [7] DEDICATION TO JOHN AND JOSEPHINE; p [8] Blank; p 9-327 Text; p [328] Blank.

5" x 7$^9$/$_{16}$". BOUND IN BLUE CLOTH; Spine Stamped in Red: SECOND | SIGHT | [Ornament] | Neil M. | Gunn | [Space] | Faber & Faber

Reprinted with a foreword by Dairmid Gunn by RICHARD DREW PUBLISHERS| GLASGOW | 1986

An Extract entitled "King Brude" comprising chapter 10 of the Novel appeared in:-

THE SCOTS MAGAZINE | DUNDEE | VOL 30 NO 5 | PP 359 - 371 | FEBRUARY 1939

The play of the same name and plot was offered to the B.B.C. and, in an accompanying letter (11.1.56) GUNN states that the novel was developed from the play.

The action centres round a shooting party in a lodge and on the hill. They are striving to shoot the legendary stag "King Brude". It is one of the gillies who has the "Second Sight" and he "sees" a funeral procession. He will not disclose the name of the victim but it is thought that this is one of the party. The reaction to this prophecy differs according to the character of the protagonists and GUNN makes full play of their differences, building to a climax at the end.

A letter to the Author from Faber dated 23.7.65 confirms the copyright had reverted to him.

A81                    (A84)

SEA COLOURS | THE SCOTS MAGAZINE | DUNDEE

VOL 34   NO 3   PP 219 - 223          DECEMBER 1940

A story of a successful fishing trip taken from the
final chapter of "The Silver Darlings" entitled "Finn
in the Heart of the Circle".


A82                    (A94)

THE LITTLE RED COW | THE SCOTS MAGAZINE | DUNDEE

VOL 34   NO 5   PP 351 - 358          FEBRUARY 1941

This story later appeared in:-

THE THISTLE AND THE PEN. Ed. ERIC LINKLATER | NELSON |
LONDON | 1950   PP 122 - 131

YOUNG ART AND OLD HECTOR | FABER & FABER | 15.3.1942 |
PP 229 - 240

The First of what were to become part of the latter
book - used as chapter 16.

The cow was being taken to market by Donul.   Both
were from up Country and found things strange.


A83              (A6, A22, A30, A115)

HENRY DRAKE GOES HOME | CHAMBERS'S JOURNAL | EDINBURGH |

8TH SERIES   VOL 10   NO 569   PP 129 - 132 MARCH 1941

This story later appeared in:-

THE WHITE HOUR | FABER & FABER | 2nd OCTOBER 1950
PP 242 - 250

This story was also offered to the B.B.C.  6.9.1940
but was not taken up.

A touching story of a Devonian old age pensioner

living in Northern Scotland who feels, during war
time, the urge to return to and see again the land of
his birth despite previous feelings of animosity.
The sympathetic Social Security Official who monitors
his journey, on foot, from reports concerning the
drawing of his pension is aware that he has arrived
home spiritually although he physically only reached
Manchester.

This may contain an autobiographical element as his
early work included pension investigations.


A84

(A69, A81, A95, A124, D167, D234, E16, E17, E18, E19,
E29, E30, E62, E63, E79, E83, E84, E90, E102, E103,
E104, E106, E107, E108, E109)

THE SILVER DARLINGS | FABER & FABER | LONDON

First Edition:-                                24TH APRIL 1941

THE | SILVER DARLINGS | by | NEIL M. GUNN | [Space] |
FABER AND FABER LIMITED | 24 Russell Square | London.

Collation:- [A]$^{16}$, B-1$^{16}$, No J, K-S$^{16}$, T$^4$. 292
Leaves.

p [1] THE SILVER DARLINGS | [ornament]; p [2] by the
same author; p [3] TITLE PAGE; p [4] [ital]
Publishers and Printers Notices: First Published in
April MCMXLI; p [5] TO | THE MEMORY OF | MY     FATHER;
p [6] Blank; p 7 Contents; p [8] Blank; p 9 - 584
Text.

5$^1$/$_8$" x 7$^3$/$_4$"; BOUND IN BLUE CLOTH; Spine Stamped in
Silver: THE | SILVER | DARLINGS | [ornament] | NEIL | GUNN
| [Space] | FABER AND | FABER.

REPRINTED FABER & FABER | LONDON | 1969

Other Editions:-

G.W.STEWART | NEW YORK | 1945

An extract entitled "Storm and Precipice" comprising part of page 307, pages 308 - 324 and part of page 325 appeared in:-

STORM AND PRECIPICE | FABER & FABER | 1ST OCT. 1942 | PP 53 - 70

A short story called "Sea Colours" which is basically an extract from the final chapter, PP 574 - 579 with some slight amendment appeared in:-

THE SCOTS MAGAZINE | DUNDEE | VOL 34 NO 3 | PP 219 - 223 | DECEMBER 1940

The Short story "The Boat" which appeared in:-

THE SCOTS MAGAZINE | DUNDEE | VOL 28 NO 3 | PP 186 - 194 | DECEMBER 1937

Was adapted to form the opening chapter.

An extract from Chapter one, used as a subject for a reading on the B.B.C. School Programme "Scottish Magazine", was printed in "B.B.C. Radio Scottish Magazine Teachers notes Spring/Summer 1978 PP 3 - 4

An extract entitled "The Herring Fishers" appeared in SCOTLAND, AN ANTHOLOGY | CADOGAN BOOKS | LONDON | 1984 | PP 83 - 86

This Novel was filmed in 1947 by the Associated British Picture Corporation.

The Novel was also adapted for Radio by John Wilson and was produced 3.9.1962 by Finlay J. MacDonald for the Scottish Home Service. A typescript of this adaptation is held at both the B.B.C. Glasgow and the

B.B.C. Script Library (Plays) London.

An article entitled "The Silver Fish" by Neil Gunn appeared in the Radio Times 30.8.62.

Neil Gunn's Father, to whose memory this novel is dedicated, was himself a fisherman.

A further radio adaptation was done by Tom McGrath and was produced in 5 episodes of 1 hour each by Tom Kinninmont in June/July 1982.

According to Prof. F.R. Hart | Neil M.Gunn: The Man and the Writer | Blackwood | EDINBURGH | 1973 | An old Dunbeath man had told GUNN of the first four men to go ˙through the Pentland Firth to the West Coast fishing - this is incorporated into the book. He also states that other historical details were recorded in a ledger dated 1815 GUNN found at Helmsdale.

This is certainly one of GUNN's more popular novels and deservedly so. It is a novel of epic proportions dealing with the rise of the herring industry.


A85                    (A115)

LOVE'S DIALECTIC | THE SCOTS MAGAZINE | DUNDEE
VOL 35  NO 2  PP 133 - 143                  MAY 1941
This story later appeared in:-
THE WHITE HOUR | FABER & FABER | 2 OCT. 1950 | PP143-157
An intricate and effective love story seen from the woman's standpoint. She is a war-time censor.


A86                    (A94)

THE FIRST RUN OF GRISLE | CHAMBERS'S JOURNAL |

EDINBURGH | 8TH SERIES

VOL 10   NO 582   PP 337 - 341                    JUNE 1941

Story later appeared in:-

YOUNG ART AND OLD HECTOR | FABER & FABER |

5TH MARCH 1942 | PP 11 - 21

The second of what were to become part of the above book but was in fact used as the first chapter.

We are introduced to the two main characters.  Young Art is disgruntled at not being allowed to go with his brother to the river to poach grilse.  Instead he begins to learn of wisdom from Old Hector through the re-telling of the story of Finn MacCoul's obtaining of wisdom by eating the Salmon of Wisdom which had fed upon the Nuts of Knowledge.  Both recurring themes in GUNN's fiction.


A87                        (A94)

THE BIRDBEAST AND THE TWELVE PUPPIES | CHAMBERS'S
JOURNAL | EDINBURGH | 8TH SERIES

VOL 10   NO 594   PP 529 - 532               SEPTEMBER 1941

This story later appeared in:-

YOUNG ART AND OLD HECTOR | FABER&FABER | 5TH MARCH 1942

PP 41 - 50 WITH THE TITLE "MACHINERY"

The third of what were to become part of the above book.  This story became Chapter Three.

Young Art and his brother Donul visit a hill, full of machinery which is somewhat frightening to the young boy.  It would seem that a still operates from the premises but on this occasion a Ceilidh is taking place.  The traditional story of "The Birdbeast and the Twelve Puppies" is recounted.


A88                         (A94)

UNDER AN OLD GOOSEBERRY BUSH | THE SCOTS MAGAZINE

| DUNDEE

VOL 36   NO 2   PP 117 - 131                NOVEMBER 1941

This story later appeared in:-

YOUNG ART AND OLD HECTOR | FABER&FABER | 5TH MARCH 1942

| PP 51 - 71

The fourth of what were to become part of the above
book.  This story became Chapter Four.

Art is despatched to stay overnight with Old Hector
due to his mother's illness.  He is reluctant and
homesick but as a diversion he is introduced into
rabbit poaching and narrowly avoids capture.  The
following day his mother is better following a
mysterious delivery in which gooseberry bushes
feature.


A89                         (A94)

THE FIRST AND SECOND CHILDHOOD | THE SCOTS MAGAZINE

| DUNDEE

VOL 36   NO 3   PP 161 - 171                DECEMBER 1941

This story later appeared in:-

YOUNG ART AND OLD HECTOR | FABER&FABER | 5TH MARCH 1942

| PP 72 - 92

The fifth of what were to become part of the above
book.  This story became Chapter Five.

Art experiences traumatic feelings in trying to
adjust to his new baby brother.  In his distress Old

Hector, said to be in his second childhood, understands best his fears and motivations.

A90                     (A94)

THE KNIFE, THE GLASS BALL AND THE PENNY |
CHAMBERS'S JOURNAL | EDINBURGH | 8TH SERIES

VOL 11   NO 611   PP 33 - 39                JANUARY 1942

This story later appeared in:-

YOUNG ART AND OLD HECTOR | FABER&FABER | 5TH MARCH 1942
| PP 22 - 40

The sixth of what were to become part of the above book. This story became Chapter Two.

Young Art discovers that life can be divided into three parts; childhood, old age and courting. For those involved in the latter, publicity is an Achilles heel - gifts and surprising and unexplained behaviour can follow.

A91                     (A94)

THE NEW JERSEY, THE FLUKE AND THE WHISPERING REEDS
| THE SCOTS MAGAZINE | DUNDEE

VOL 36   NO 4   PP 270 - 280                JANUARY 1942

This story later appeared in :-

YOUNG ART AND OLD HECTOR | FABER&FABER | 5TH MARCH 1942
| PP 93 - 108

The seventh of what were to become part of the above book. This story became Chapter Six.

A further incident in the life of Young Art in which he acknowledges that he is fond of his baby brother.

A92                    (A94, A95, E23)

  ART RUNS A GREAT RACE | THE SCOTS MAGAZINE | DUNDEE

VOL 36   NO 5   PP 341 - 350                FEBRUARY 1942

This story later appeared in:-

YOUNG ART AND OLD HECTOR | FABER & FABER | 5TH      MARCH

1942 | PP 131 - 145

STORM AND PRECIPICE | FABER & FABER | 1ST    OCT.    1942

PP 39 - 52

The eighth of what were to become parts of the above

book.  This story became Chapter Nine.

Art visits the local fair and sports; a red letter

day in the community.


A93                    (A94)

  NOWHERE AND SOMEWHERE | THE SCOTS MAGAZINE | DUNDEE

VOL 36   NO 6   PP 430 - 434                 MARCH 1942

This story later appeared in:-

YOUNG ART AND OLD HECTOR | FABER&FABER | 5TH  MARCH  1942

| PP 109 - 115

The ninth of what were to become parts of the above

book.  This story became Chapter Seven.

Art receives a first lesson in metaphysics.


A94          (A40, A95, A102, A121, E23)

   YOUNG ART AND OLD HECTOR | FABER & FABER | LONDON

                                    5TH  MARCH  1942

First Edition:-

YOUNG ART AND OLD HECTOR | by | NEIL M. GUNN | [space] |

FABER AND FABER LIMITED | 24 Russell Square | London.

Collation:- [A]8, B-18, No J, K-Q8, 128 Leaves

p [1] [ital] YOUNG ART AND OLD HECTOR; p [2] by the same author; p [3] TITLE PAGE; p [4] [ital] Publishers and Printers Notices: First published in MCMXLII; p [5] for | THE WOMAN OF THE HOUSE; p [6] Blank; p 7 Author's Note; p [8] Blank; p 9 Contents; p [10] Blank; p 11 - 255 Text; p [256] Blank.

5" x $7^9/_{16}$". BOUND IN BROWN CLOTH; Spine Stamped in Gold : Young | Art | & | Old | Hector | [two lines - horizontal] | Neil M. | Gunn | [space] | Faber and | Faber.

Reprinted by:- SOUVENIR PRESS LTD | LONDON | 1976

CONTENTS

I Appeared in Chambers Magazine

＊ Appeared in the Scots Magazine.

The Chapter entitled "ART RUNS A GREAT RACE" appeared in:-

STORM AND PRECIPICE | FABER & FABER | 1ST OCT. 1942 | PP 39 - 52

The Chapter entitled "THE LITTLE RED COW" appeared in:-

THE THISTLE AND THE PEN. Ed. ERIC LINKLATER | NELSON | LONDON | 1950 | PP 122 - 131

The Chapter entitled "MACHINERY" appeared as "THE BIRDBEAST AND THE TWELVE PUPPIES" in Chambers's Magazine.

A delightful book concerning the friendship and exchange of knowledge between an old man and a young boy in a Highland crofting setting. Young Art and Old Hector were to be the main protagonists in the later, and perhaps more famous, "Green Isle of the Great Deep"

According to Prof. Hart in | Neil M. Gunn: The Man and The Writer | Blackwood | Edinburgh | 1973, GUNN was himself the star runner at the local games so the Chapter "Art Runs a Great Race" at least is probably partially autobiographical.


A95        (A14,A30,A32,A42,A46,A52,A53,A57,A59,A68,A71,
            A77,A84,A92,A94,A100,A115,E18,E30,E83)
        STORM AND PRECIPICE | FABER & FABER | LONDON

                                    1ST OCTOBER 1942

First Edition:-

STORM AND PRECIPICE | and other pieces | by | NEIL M.
GUNN | [space] | FABER AND FABER LTD | 24 Russell Square
London

Collation:-[A]$^8$, B-1$^8$, No J, K$^8$  80 Leaves

p [1] STORM AND PRECIPICE | AND OTHER PIECES |
[ornament]; p [2] Blank; p [3] TITLE PAGE; p [4]
[ital] Publishers and Printers Notices: First
published in September MCMXLII | STATEMENT RE ECONOMY
STANDARDS; p 5 Contents; p 6 Contents Cont. and
Select Bibliography; p 7 - 159 Text; p [160] Blank.
4$^7/_8$" x 7$^1/_2$".  BOUND IN FAWN CLOTH; Spine stamped in
Red: (Printed vertically - Top to Bottom)
STORM AND PRECIPICE | NEIL M. GUNN | [space] | (Printed
Horizontally) FABER.

The publication date is quoted as September 1942 but
the publishers advise me that the date was 1.10.1942.
This small book contains a selection of prose
passages from books published by Faber/Porpoise.


A96      (A112, A130, B21, E9, E10, E33, E71)
    SUN AND MOON | THE SCOTS MAGAZINE | DUNDEE
VOL 38  NO 2  PP 83 - 99            NOVEMBER 1942
Story was offered for Broadcasting 22.10.42.  and was
later dramatised and produced.

A story set in wartime around the Western Isles in
which the captain of a fast patrol boat, on the look
out for U-Boats, observes the traditions of the local
islanders with regard to the sun and moon;
traditions full of respect, not paganism.

This story was later incorporated into the novel "The

Lost Chart".

A97                    (A65, A115)

  THE LISTENERS TALE | THE SCOTS MAGAZINE | DUNDEE

VOL 38   NO 3   PP 187 - 195              DECEMBER 1942

This story later appeared in:-

THE WHITE HOUR | FABER & FABER | 2ND OCT. 1950 |

PP 167 - 176

The listener re-tells a discussion which has taken
place between his friends, one setting out Freudian
arguments which are being opposed by a Socialist
Anthropologist.   GUNN obviously does not entirely
favour Freud's theories.

A98        (A6, A22, A30, A43, C5, C9, D72)
           THE SERPENT | FABER & FABER | LONDON

                                 4TH JUNE 1943

First Edition:-

THE SERPENT | by | NEIL M. GUNN | [space] |

FABER AND FABER | 24 Russell Square | London

Collation:- [A]$^8$, B-I$^8$, No J, K-Q$^8$, 128 Leaves

p [1] (ital) The Serpent | p [2] By the same author; p

[3] TITLE PAGE; p [4] for | Keith and Helen Henderson

| [space] | [ital] Publishers and Printers Notices:

First published in MCMXLIII | STATEMENT RE ECONOMY

STANDARDS; p 5 - [256] Text.

5" x 7$^1/_2$".   BOUND IN TURQUOISE CLOTH; Spine stamped

in Gold: THE | SERPENT | [double horizontal line] | NEIL

M. | GUNN | [ornament] | [space] | FABER.

Later Editions:-

With Title "MAN GOES ALONE" | G.W. STEWART | NEW YORK | 1944

CLUB LEABHAR | INVERNESS | 1969

SOUVENIR PRESS LTD | LONDON | 1978

A letter to the Author from Faber dd 23.7.65 confirms that the copyright had reverted to him.

The Highland action of this book is set near Brae where Neil Gunn did much of his writing.

The story of Tom, "The Philosopher" covering his youth in Glasgow in the 1880's and his return to his Highland home. On his return he tends to be feared and shunned by his friends due to his atheism and socialistic beliefs. This is particularly felt by Tom's father, a pillar of the Kirk, and antagonisms are created. With time the fear dwindles and Tom becomes merely "The Philosopher". The story is told in recollection form by the old man and reaches a symbolic ending.

A99                    (A115)

THE TAX GATHERER | THE SCOTS MAGAZINE | DUNDEE

VOL 39  NO 5  PP 333 - 340              AUGUST 1943

This story later appeared in:-

THE WHITE HOUR | FABER & FABER | 2ND OCT. 1950 |
PP 69 - 79

NEW PENGUIN BOOK OF SCOTTISH SHORT STORIES Ed. IAN MURRAY | PENGUIN | 1983 | PP 187 - 195

A young civil servant's dilemma in being caught between two stools. He feels the warmth of human sympathy towards people against whom, as an official, he has to take action.  The story brings out the inhumanities of the legal system with, perhaps overdone, overtones of Pontius Pilate.  In his early work GUNN conducted old age pension investigations, and one wonders whether to some extent he is expressing a personal dilemma.

From correspondence it would appear that a translation appeared circa 1957 in a German Magazine.

A100        (A40, A68, A95, E80, E85, E100)
            HIGHLAND RIVER | ARGOSY | LONDON
VOL 4   NO 7   PP 13 - 24                    AUGUST 1943
A reprinting of the first chapter of the novel of the same name published by The Porpoise Press in 1937.
The story of young Kenn's tremendous battle with a large salmon in a pool.

A101                    (A115)
        THE CHARIOT | THE SCOTS MAGAZINE | DUNDEE
VOL 40   NO 3   PP 167 - 179                  DECEMBER 1943
This story later appeared in:-
THE WHITE HOUR | FABER & FABER | 2ND OCT. 1950 |
PP 11 - 27
GUNN here explores the same theme as that of "The White Hour" but with a difference in the character and attitude of the central figure who is approaching death.  As opposed to a warm outward feeling there is here a cold attitude and a terrible loneliness.  In the end life however must continue.  Here, I believe, GUNN is obliquely commenting upon the modern

pecuniarily based society as against the old co-operative spirit.

A102        (A23, A94, E79, E91, E92, E99, E110)
THE GREEN ISLE OF THE GREAT DEEP | FABER & FABER | LONDON

6TH JUNE 1944

First Edition:-

The Green Isle | of the Great Deep | by | Neil M. Gunn | [space] | Faber and Faber Limited | 24 Russell Square | London.

Collation:-[A]$^8$, B-1$^8$, No J, K-Q$^8$, 128 Leaves

p [1] THE GREEN ISLE | OF THE GREAT DEEP | For Old Hector | and others like him | who were friendly | to many a Highland boy, | this phantasy; p [2] By The Same Author; p [3] TITLE PAGE; p [4] [ital] Publishers and Printers Notices : First published in MCMXLIV | [space] | STATEMENT RE ECONOMY STANDARDS; p 5-6 Contents; p 7-256 Text.

5" x 7$^1/_2$". BOUND IN DARK GREEN CLOTH; Spine Stamped in Gold: [Three Wavy Horizontal Lines] | The | Green | Isle | of | the | Great | Deep | [Three Wavy Horizontal Lines] | Neil | M. | Gunn | [Three Wavy Horizontal Lines] | [space] | F & F.

Later Edition:-

SOUVENIR PRESS LTD | LONDON | 1975

Later adapted for Radio and Broadcast 22.1.1966.

The main characters in this novel are Young Art and Old Hector from an earlier novel of that title. The book, which GUNN in his dedication refers to as a phantasy, commences with a trip to the river which had been Art's aim in the earlier book. From there they are mystically transported to "The Green Isle", The Celtic TIR NAN OG, but all is not well as God has been asleep. The book concerns Art and Hector's rebellion against the hierarchy who run the "Green Isle" in God's absence. The book is a most unusual one in many ways but retains GUNN's central belief in the individual. As such it is a commentary on the dangers inherent in a totalitarian state.

Dr. Robert MacIntyre of the S.N.P. recalls a conversation with GUNN and quotes his reply to the question "Why is the Green Isle of the Great Deep not better known?" as "I don't know, it was my best book".


A103                          (A109)

CONVALESCENCE | THE SCOTS MAGAZINE | DUNDEE

VOL 42   NO 1   PP 1 - 13                    OCTOBER 1944

This short story, slightly amended, became Chapter I of Part I of "The Shadow". The whole of Part I in the book bore the same title.

A young girl who has suffered a nervous breakdown in the city is convalescing in the Highlands. The story is a record of her feelings and observations in the form of letters to her boyfriend.


A104                          (A115, A126)

PURE CHANCE | THE SCOTS MAGAZINE | DUNDEE

VOL 42   NO 6   PP 452 - 468                  MARCH 1945

This story later appeared in:-

THE WHITE HOUR | FABER & FABER | 2ND OCT. 1950 |
PP 192 - 213

A strange psychological thriller with more than a
touch of the occult. It centres around a Gaelic song
which seems to have an unwelcome effect upon its
performers, but of course it could be pure chance!
In some of the incidents recounted and the dialogue
there is a foretaste of "The Other Landscape".

A105                    (A49, A126)

THE KEY OF THE CHEST | FABER & FABER | LONDON

26TH JANUARY 1946

First Edition:-

THE KEY | OF THE CHEST | by | NEIL M. GUNN | [space] |
FABER AND FABER | 24 Russell Square | London

Collation:- [A]$^{16}$, B-G$^{16}$, H$^2$, H*$^{14}$, R$^4$, 132 Leaves
p [1] THE KEY | OF THE CHEST ; p [2] By the Same
Author; p [3] TITLE PAGE; p [4] FOR | PETER AND ENA |
[space] | [ital] Publishers and Printers Notices :
First published in MCMXLV | STATEMENT RE ECONOMY
STANDARDS; p 5 - 262 Text; p [263]-[264] Blank
5" x 7$^1$/$_2$". BOUND IN BLUE COTH; Spine Stamped in
Gold: [Three Horizontal Lines] | THE | KEY | OF | THE |
CHEST | [Three Horizontal Lines] | NEIL | M. | GUNN |
[Three Horizontal Lines] | [space] | F & F.

Later Editions:-

Reprinted by CEDRIC CHIVERS LTD | BATH | 1966   at   the
request of the London and Home Counties Branch of the
Library Association.

G.W. STEWART | NEW YORK | 1946

This work bears the imprint 1945 but was not in fact published, according to Faber, until 26th January 1946.

This novel is based largely on the short story "The Dead Seaman" which appeared in the Scots Magazine in July 1931.

A mystery of a dead seaman who is suspected of being murdered by a local shepherd who lives physically and metaphorically outside the village.

The copyright has been transferred to Cedric Chivers Ltd.


A106                          (A107)

   A DREAM OF EDINBURGH | THE SCOTS MAGAZINE | DUNDEE

VOL 45   NO 5   PP 343 - 348                AUGUST 1946

An extract from "The Drinking Well" which was published 21.2.1947 although bearing the imprint 1946.


A107   (A24,A33,A34,A40,A51,A106,B5,E4,E11,E12,E36,E58,
                        E77)

       THE DRINKING WELL | FABER & FABER | LONDON

                              21ST FEBRUARY 1947

First Edition:-

THE | DRINKING WELL | by | NEIL M. GUNN | [space] |
FABER AND FABER LTD. | 24 Russell Square | London

Collation:- [A]$^8$, B-I$^{16}$, NO J, K-P$^{16}$.   232 Leaves

p [1] THE DRINKING WELL; p [2] By the Same Author;

p [3] TITLE PAGE; p [4] [ital] Publishers and

Printers Notices: First published in MCMXLVI; p 5
Contents; p [6] TO MY | OLD FRIEND IAN | and the sheep
farm on the Grampians, | not forgetting the little
black diary; p [7] PART 1 | AT HOME ; p [8] Blank; p 9
- 464 Text.

5" x 7$^1/_2$". BOUND IN GREEN CLOTH; Spine stamped in
Gold: THE | DRINKING | WELL | BY | NEIL M. | GUNN | [space]
| FABER.

Later Editions:-

G.W. STEWART | NEW YORK | 1947

SOUVENIR PRESS LTD | LONDON | 1978

Whilst this work bears the imprint 1946 it was,
according to Faber, not published until 21st February
1947.

Some copies of the first edition are known to have
been mis-bound with two "M" Sections and no "N"
Section.

Iain Cattenach, The Hero, first appeared in "The Man
Who Came Back (Study for a one-act play)" in The
Scots Magazine | Dundee | March 1928 and again in the
one-act play, "Back Home", W. Wilson | Glasgow | 1932

An extract entitled "A Dream of Edinburgh" comprising
Chapter 15 of Part 2 of the Novel (with slight
alterations) appeared in:-

THE SCOTS MAGAZINE | DUNDEE | AUGUST 1946 | PP343 - 348

An extract entitled "Poaching" comprising part of
Page 57, Pages 58-59 and part of Page 60 of the Novel
appeared in:-

SCOTLAND - AN ANTHOLOGY Ed. MAURICE LINDSAY | ROBERT
HALE | NOVEMBER 1974

The work was dramatised for Radio and produced
3.12.1956.

The Film Rights were sold to Ealing Studios Ltd who
did not proceed.

The story explores, in much greater depth the ideas
first expressed in "Back Home" and shows as well the
contrasts between urban and rural life.

The rural setting is a large sheep farm between
Newtonmore and Dalwhinnie in the Grampians and which
was known to GUNN.


A108                         (A115)

       ON THE STONE | THE SCOTS MAGAZINE | DUNDEE
VOL 46   NO 5   PP 333 - 344             FEBRUARY 1947
This story later appeared in:-
THE WHITE HOUR | FABER & FABER | 2ND OCT. 1950 |
PP104-117
ARGOSY | LONDON | VOL 12 | NO 1 | JANUARY 1951 |
PP 123 - 132
The story of two young persons, in love and inwardly
shy.   They come together at the end of the story
having physically being on the edge of disaster.


A109                      (A72, A103)

        THE SHADOW | FABER & FABER | LONDON

                          20TH FEBRUARY 1948
First Edition:-
THE SHADOW | by | NEIL M. GUNN | [space] |
FABER AND FABER LIMITED | 24 Russell Square | London
Collation:- [A]8, B-H16. 120 Leaves.

p [1] THE SHADOW; p [2] By The Same Author; p [3] TITLE PAGE; p [4] [ital] Publishers and Printers Notices: First published in MCMXLVIII; p [5] Contents; p [6] FOR | JOHN AND GENE; p 7 - 240 Text.

5" x $7^1/_2$". BOUND IN RED CLOTH; Spine Stamped in Gold: [ornament] | The | Shadow | [ornament] | Neil M. Gunn | [space] | Faber.

The short story "Convalescence", which appeared in the Scots Magazine | Dundee | October 1944 | PP 1 - 13, became, with slight amendments, Chapter one of Part one of the Novel. Part One is similarily entitled "Convalescence".

A letter to the Author from Faber dd 23.7.65 confirms that the Copyright had reverted to him.

The action in the novel is set in the countryside round Brae where GUNN lived 1938 - 1948

The short story "Snow in March" | The Scots Magazine | Dundee | June 1938 | PP 191 - 199 is also worked into the plot as a dramatic interlude.

A complex story of a young girl's mental breakdown, convalescence and fight to recover.


A110        (A4, A15, A50, A119, A130, E13)
            THE SILVER BOUGH | FABER & FABER | LONDON
                                    22ND OCTOBER 1948

First Edition:-

THE SILVER BOUGH | by | NEIL M. GUNN | [space] |
FABER AND FABER | 24 Russell Square | London

Collation:- [A]8, Bb-Ib8, No Jb, Kb-Sb8, Tb2, Tb*10, Ub8, 164 Leaves.

[...] Blank; p [3] THE SILVER BOUGH; p [4] By The
Same Author; p [5] TITLE-PAGE; p [6] [ital]
Publishers and Printers Notices: First Published in
MCMXLVIII; p [7] To the memory of | JOHN ROSE FREW; p
[8] Blank, p 9 - 328 Text.

5" x 7$\frac{1}{2}$".   BOUND IN BLUE CLOTH; Spine stamped in Gold:
THE | SILVER | BOUGH | by | NEIL M. GUNN | (space) FABER.
Reprinted with a foreword by Dairmid Gunn by RICHARD DREW
PUBLISHERS | GLASGOW | 1985.

This novel is based on the short story "The Circle", which
appeared in:-

THE SCOTS MAGAZINE | DUNDEE | JAN 1932 | PP 241 - 255

Two other of GUNN's short stories, which were not
published to my knowledge, contain a sea rescue
episode virtually identical to that in "The Silver
Bough".   It seems probable that these preceded the
Novel but it is not possible to verify this from the
addresses on the manuscript.   These are:-

The Face in the Pool (address Kincraig 1948 - 50)

The Terrible Ally (Address Kerrow House, Cannich 1950
- 60)

John Rose Frew, to whom the book is dedicated was
Neil Gunn's father-in-law.

See Note under "The Circle"


A111

FOOTSTEPS IN THE CORRIDOR | UNPUBLISHED

FROM ADDRESS 1938-1948

Typescript held at the National Library of Scotland.

An intellectual love story bearing the philosophical
stamp and more indirect and convoluted approach of

70

A112    (A96, A130, B21, E9, E10, E33, E71)

THE LOST CHART | FABER & FABER | LONDON

10TH MAY 1949

First Edition:-

THE LOST CHART | by | NEIL M. GUNN | [space] |

FABER AND FABER LIMITED | 24 Russell Square | London

Collation:- [A]$^8$, B-I$^8$, No J, K-U$^8$, No V&W, X-Y$^8$,176 Leaves.

p [1] THE LOST CHART; p [2] By the Same Author; p [3] TITLE PAGE; p [4] [ital] Publishers and Printers Notices: First Published MCMXLIX; p 5-352 Text.

5" x 7$^1/_2$". BOUND IN BLUE CLOTH; Spine Stamped in Gold: (in decorative Scroll: THE | LOST | CHART | )    a novel by | NEIL M. | GUNN | [space] | FABER

REPRINTED BY RICHARD DREW PUBLISHERS | GLASGOW | 1987 Part of the story "Sun and Moon" which appeared in the Scots Magazine | Dundee | Nov. 1942 | PP 123 - 126 was utilised in this story.

The above story was dramatised by GUNN for Radio and was first broadcast 1.6.1944.

During the Second World War GUNN was in charge of shipping and routing ships round mine fields on the West Coast of Scotland. He reported to and was instructed by the Admiralty at Kinlochleven. He has drawn on his war time experiences in this novel.

The Lost Chart is a complicated story of espionage and counter-espionage set in the cold war period of the later 1940's.


A113

(A78, A133, B15, B22, C9, D32, D39, D71, D72, D73,

..., A133, B15, B22, C9, D32, D39, D71, D72, D73, D74, D75, D77, D79, D82, D84, D86, D87, D89, D93, D95, D98, D100, D102, D103, D105, D107, D108, D109, D110, D112, D116, D118, D120, D121, D122, D123, D124, D125, D128, D129, D131, D132, D134, D136, D139, D140, D141, D142, D144, D187, D189)

HIGHLAND PACK | FABER & FABER | LONDON

18TH NOVEMBER 1949

First Edition:-

HIGHLAND PACK | by | NEIL GUNN | With drawings by | KEITH HENDERSON | [space] | [Illustrations] FABER AND FABER LIMITED | 24 Russell Square | London

Collation:- [A]$^8$, B-I$^8$, No J, K-Q$^8$, R$^1$, R*$^9$, 138 Leaves

p [1]-[2] Blank, p [3](ital) HIGHLAND PACK; p [4] By the Same Author; p [5] TITLE PAGE; p [6] [ital] Publishers and Printers Notices: First published in MCMXLIX; p [7] For | THE GARDENER; p [8] Blank; p 9-11 FOREWORD; p [12] Blank; p 13 ACKNOWLEDGEMENTS: THE GLASGOW HERALD, S.M.T. MAGAZINE AND CHAMBERS'S JOURNAL; p [14] Blank; p 15 - 16 Contents; p 17-274 Text; p [275]-[276] Blank.


5 $^3/_8$" x 8 $^1/_8$". BOUND IN RED CLOTH; Spine stamped in Gold: [Three Horizontal Lines] | HIGH- | LAND | PACK | [Three Horizontal Lines] | NEIL | M. | GUNN | [Space] | FABER

This book is mainly a collection of nature stories

appeared in the Scots Magazine as is acknowledged in the Foreword. These were written under the pseudonym of Dane McNeil and were published under the general headings of "Memories of the Month" and "A Countryman's Year".

Chapter 7 was based on an article "The Mole-Catcher" in The Glasgow Herald | Glasgow | 10th May 1941 | P.3.

Chapter 35 was based on an article "In The Wilds of Sutherland" in the S.M.T. Magazine | Edinburgh | July 1940 | PP 22 - 27

Chapter 47 was based on an article "The Factor's Tale" in the Glasgow Herald | Glasgow | 9TH MAR. 1940 | P.3. Chapters 48 - 53 were based on a series in Chambers's Journal | Edinburgh entitled "Islands and Seas" and comprising:-

I    From Stornoway to Bernera | Feb 1940 | PP 103 - 107
II   Farewell to Bernera | Mar 1940 | PP 204 - 207
III  To the Flannan Isles | Apr 1940 | PP 285 - 288
IV   The Light That Failed | May 1940 | PP 348 - 351

The Gardener to whom this book is dedicated is GUNN's Wife.

According to Prof. F.R. Hart in | Neil M. Gunn: The Man and the Writer | Blackwood | Edinburgh | 1973, it was Malcolm MacLeod who took GUNN to Bernera. Malcolm lived in Stornoway and had once been a member of Neil Gunn's Father's Crew.

Part of Chapter 34, "The Gentle Rain From Heaven" comprising pages 162 - 166 was later collected in:-
REFLECTIONS | RONALD THOMSON | THURSO | 1978 | PP 10 - 12

Chapter 31, "The Rose at the Gable End"
comprising pages 145 - 149 was later collected in:-
REFLECTIONS | RONALD THOMSON | THURSO | 1978 | PP 18 - 20

A114

GOLD COMES BY CHANCE | THE GLASGOW HERALD | GLASGOW
P 3                                    15TH APRIL 1950
A short story of a young hitch hiker's chance meeting
with a shepherd and the spiritually enriching moments
which followed.

A115

THE WHITE HOUR | FABER & FABER | LONDON
                              2ND OCTOBER 1950
First Edition:-
THE WHITE HOUR | and other stories | [ornament] | NEIL
M. GUNN | [space] | FABER AND FABER LTD |
24 Russell Square | London
Collation:- [A]$^8$, B-I$^8$, No J, K-S$^8$, 144 Leaves.
p [1] - [2] Blank; p [3] The White Hour; p [4] By the
Same Author; p [5] TITLE-PAGE; p [6] [ital]
Publishers and Printers Notices: First published in
MCML; p 7 - 8 Contents; p 9 NOTE (Acknowledgments to
"The Scots Magazine", "Chambers's Journal",
"Cornhill", "Dublin Magazine", "Scotland's Magazine",
"Scottish Field" and "Spectator"; p [10] Blank; p 11
- 285 Text; p [286] - [288] Blank.
5" x 7$^1$/$_2$".   BOUND IN BEIGE CLOTH; Spine Stamped in
Gold: THE | WHITE | HOUR | [ornament] | NEIL M. | GUNN |
[space] | FABER.

74

...tion of the undermentioned short stories:-

I    Also Appear in "STORM AND PRECIPICE" 1942 A95

*    Also appear in "HIDDEN DOORS" 1930 A42

The  Short  Story  "The  Black  Woollen  Gloves"  was

...ed for Radio and first produced 8.2.1944.    I
have been unable to trace a previous publication of:-
"The Ghost's Story"
"The Telegram"
The Former was however offered to the B.B.C. for
Broadcasting 3.6.1940 but was declined.
The Latter, from Correspondence, appears to have been
Published in a Danish Magazine "Magasinet" around
August 1956.


A116                     (A40, A121)
 PRIMITIVES IN THE POOL | THE GLASGOW HERALD | GLASGOW
P 3                               28TH OCTOBER 1950
This Story later appeared in:-
CASUAL COLUMNS | GEORGE OUTRAM & CO LTD | GLASGOW | 1955
| PP 148 - 151
Husband and wife on a salmon poaching expedition
which came about by chance.  The Story was used again
in the early part of "The Well at the Worlds End".
From correspondence quoted by Prof. F.R. Hart in his
essay for | Neil M. Gunn: The Man and the Writer |
Blackwood | Edinburgh | 1973, it is clear this is
autobiographical.


A117          (A40, A80, B2, B14, B23)
        THE LOST WOMAN | HOLIDAY | PHILADELPHIA
VOL 8  NO 4  PP 60 - 63, 112, 114, 115   OCTOBER 1950
This story was offered to "Argosy", unsuccessfully.
Set in a Deer Forest during the stalking season this
story concerns a Scots woman desired by two men; one

, ᴄᴴᴱ oᴄher American. In this instance –
intended for the U.S. Market, the American wins.
There are clear parallels with "Second Sight" and
"Poaching at Grianan" and with his three act plays
"Second Sight", "The Ancient Fire" and "Beyond The
Cage".

All8          (A25, A35, A60, A121)
          RIDE THE GALE | THE SATURDAY EVENING POST |
                    PHILADELPHIA
VOL 223  NO 25  PP 20-21, 104-106  16TH DECEMBER 1950
This story later appeared in:-
ARGOSY | LONDON | VOL 12  NO 3  PP 5 - 16  MARCH 1951
A brilliant short story of a storm at sea and the
pride of an old sailing boat skipper.  It tells of
his battle with the elements.
The story was adapted from the earlier short story
"The Storm" which appeared in The Scots Magazine in
Feb. 1935.  It was later used as an episode in "The
Well at the Worlds End".

All9  (A34, A40, A45, A51, A110, A130, B2, B23)
          THE FACE IN THE POOL | UNPUBLISHED
               From Address  1948 - 1950
Typescript held at the National Library of Scotland.
A story full of vitality as in his early work.  It
is in the nature of a romance between a young
fisherman, living with his widowed mother, and
Isobel, the Laird's daughter.  (The use of these
semi-hopeless liaisons is widespread in GUNN's Work –

77

...e Lost Glen", "Poaching at Grianan", "The Ancient Fire", "Beyond The Cage" etc.) The opening paragraph illustrates the title in a passage reminiscent of "Sea Tangle". The Laird is interested in Archaeology/Geology, as in "The Silver Bough" and is trapped in a cave by the rising tide whilst digging out a fossil. The hero rescues him by boat after a daring row and is suitably rewarded. This latter scene is almost a carbon copy of the rescue in "The Silver Bough".

A120                    (A121)
         IN A SPANISH GARDEN | ARGOSY | LONDON
VOL 12   NO 4   PP 97 - 104                    APRIL 1951
An unusual story of Scots on holiday in Spain and of a swim which almost became a tragedy. This story was told by one of the group operating the illicit still in the novel "The Well at the Worlds End".

A121
     (A25, A35, A60, A94, A116, A118, A120, B21, D178,
               D242, E14, E94, E96)
    THE WELL AT THE WORLD'S END | FABER & FABER | LONDON
                         26TH OCTOBER 1951
First Edition:-
The Well | At The World's End | by | NEIL M. GUNN |
[SPACE] | FABER & FABER LIMITED | 24 Russell Square |
London
Collation:- [A]$^8$, B-I$^8$, NO J, K-Q$^8$, R$^2$, R$*^{10}$, S$^8$, 148 Leaves.

p [1] THE WELL AT THE WORLD'S END; p [2] By The Same Author; p [3] TITLE-PAGE; p [4] [ital] Publishers and Printers Notices: First published in MCMLI; p [5] for | R.M.M.; p [6] Blank; P 7 - [295] Text; p [296] Blank.

5" x $7^1/2$".  BOUND IN BLUE CLOTH; Spine Stamped in Gold: THE | WELL | AT THE | WORLD'S | END | [ornament] | NEIL | M. | GUNN | [Space] | FABER.

Later Editions:-

Reprinted at the request of the London and Home Counties Branch of the Library Association by:-

CEDRIC CHIVERS LTD | BATH | 1968

SOUVENIR PRESS | LONDON | 1985

Dramatised for Radio and first produced in Three Episodes, 28.2.70, 7.3.70 and 14.3.70.

This novel draws more heavily on GUNN's other work than any.  The opening chapter follows closely "The Pursuit of Light" | Scotlands Magazine | Edinburgh | April 1950 | PP 38 - 41, and it is clearly autobiographical as is the action of chapter three. This is based on "Primitives in the Pool" | The Glasgow Herald | Glasgow | 28.10.1950 | P  3.  The undermentioned short stories were also incorporated as interludes in the novel:-

The Storm | Scots Magazine | Dundee | Feb 1935 | PP 349 - 357

In a Spanish Garden | Argosy | London | Apr 1951 | PP 97 - 104

"The Storm" was itself re-written and published as "Ride the Gale" in:-

SATURDAY EVENING POST | PHILADELPHIA | 16TH DEC. 1950 |
PP 20 - 21, 104 - 106

ARGOSY | LONDON | MARCH 1951 | PP 5 - 16

The incident of the illicit still has also similarities to episodes in "Whisky and Scotland", "Young Art and Old Hector" and the later, unpublished, film script "The Water Of Life".

The understanding wife in the Novel, "FAND", has been identified as GUNN's wife.

Cocklebuster of the novel was described as being the character GUNN had most fully visualised and is based on a person he had met in the period 1911 - 21.

The conception "The Well at the World's End" owes something to Connla's Well of Celtic Mythology - See F.R. Hart in | Neil M. Gunn: The Man and the Writer | Blackwood | Edinburgh | 1973.

This is a very symbolic novel concerning the search for truth and the inner self by a Professor of History on holiday in the Scottish Highlands. There is more than a hint of the thinking which was to be set out later in "The Atom of Delight".

An article "Strange Happenings in the Highlands", being a conversation between GUNN and Deirdre MacDonald appears in the Radio Times (Scottish Edition) | London | Vol 186 | No 2416 | P 12 | 26th February 1970.

A122

REVOLUTION IN THE HIGHLANDS | THE GLASGOW HERALD |

P 3                                    12TH JULY 1952

This story later appeared in:-

CASUAL COLUMNS | GEORGE OUTRAM & CO LTD | GLASGOW |

1955 | PP 9 - 13

Typescript held at the National Library of Scotland.

This story is used as a vehicle for illustrating the

coming of electricity to the Highlands.


A123            (A26, A128, E20, E48, E66)

          BLOODHUNT | FABER & FABER | LONDON

                           26TH   SEPTEMBER   1952

First Edition:-

BLOODHUNT | [ornamental horizontal line] | NEIL M.   GUNN

| [Space] | FABER AND FABER LTD | 24 Russell Square |

London

Collation:- [A]$^8$, B-I$^8$, NO J, K-Q$^8$, 128 Leaves

p [1] - [2] Blank; p[3] BLOODHUNT; p [4] By The

Same  Author;  p  [5]  TITLE  PAGE;  p  [6]  [ital]

Publishers and Printers Notices: First published in

MCMLII; p [7] FOR R.W.; p [8] Blank; p 9 - 250 Text;

p [251] - [256] Blank.

5" x 7$^1$/$_2$".   BOUND  IN  RED  CLOTH;  Spine  stamped  in

Gold:  BLOOD | HUNT | [ornament] | NEIL M. | GUNN |

[Space] | FABER

Reprinted by:-

SOUVENIR PRESS | LONDON | 1984

This  novel  was  dramatised  for  Radio  and  produced

28.4.1958.

A  letter  to  the  Author  from  Faber  dd  23.7.65

confirms that the copyright had reverted to him.

The "R.W" of the dedication is Robert Wotherspoon.

The action of this book is set in the countryside near Brae, GUNN's home from 1938 - 1948.

There were foreshadowings of some of the themes explored in this novel in the short story "Birdsong at Evening" | The Cornhill | London | September 1926 | PP 298 - 314

A good exciting thriller of murder and a manhunt; against that background GUNN introduces us to some memorable people, archtypal characters, and explores motivation and morality in more than purely legal terms.


A124                    (A84)

DESPERATE JOURNEY | THE SATURDAY EVENING POST |

PHILADELPHIA

VOL 225  NO 23  PP 30, 90, 92, 97, 98, 103, 105

6TH  DECEMBER  1952

This story later appeared in:-

THE SATURDAY EVENING POST STORIES 1952 | THE   SATURDAY EVENING POST | NEW YORK | 1952 | PP 180 - 196

YOUTH AND THE FUTURE | PRENTICE-HALL | NEW JERSEY | 1959 | PP 164 - 175

This short story bore the two working titles of:-

"All One Family" and "I've Got To Get Through".

The story of an isolated keeper and his family.  His son falls ill during a particularly bad winter spell and he has to make a hazardous journey to obtain help.  A similar theme to the "Trial by Plague" passage of "The Silver Darlings". The writing and words seem uncharacteristic no doubt due to its having been written for the American market.


A125

COUNTRYMAN AT THE PLAY | THE GLASGOW HERALD | GLASGOW

P 3                                    13TH DECEMBER 1952

A dissertation on modern writers by an old countryman who is watching a play by George Bernard Shaw.


A126            (A28, A104, A105, E22)

THE OTHER LANDSCAPE | FABER & FABER | LONDON

5TH MARCH 1954

First Edition:-

The Other Landscape | by | NEIL M. GUNN | [Space] |
FABER AND FABER | 24 Russell Square | London

Collation:- [A]$^8$, B-I$^8$, NO J, K-U$^8$, 160 Leaves

p [1] - [2] Blank; p [3] THE OTHER LANDSCAPE; p [4]
By The Same Author; p [5] TITLE-PAGE; p [6]
[ital] Publishers and Printers Notices: First
published in MCMLIV; p 7 - 318 Text; p [319] - [320]
Blank.

5" x 7$^1$/$_2$". BOUND IN GREEN CLOTH; Spine Stamped in
Blue: [Two Horizontal Parentheses] | THE | OTHER | LAND-
| SCAPE | [Two Horizontal Parentheses] | NEIL | M. | GUNN
| [Space] | FABER

The character of the major in this novel is based on
a person GUNN met in the period 1911 - 21 - See
F.R. Hart | Neil M. Gunn: The Man and the Writer |

Blackwood | Edinburgh | 1973.

In the novel the character Douglas Menzies scales a sea cliff in a manner reminiscent of the shepherd in "The Key of the Chest".

The narrator of the book has been commissioned to ascertain the facts behind a manuscript of a story called "Cliffs" submitted to a publisher friend. He visits the author, a virtual recluse since the death of his wife, and strikes up a friendship. The author has become obsessed with the "Other Landscape" or supernatural landscape behind the visible one. A highly complex novel which, nevertheless, contains humorous passages.


A127  (A40, B27, D207, D208, D214, D215, D216, D219,
       D221, D232, D240, D241, E37, E41, E57, E79, F16)
       THE ATOM OF DELIGHT | FABER & FABER | LONDON
                                        12TH OCTOBER 1956

First Edition:-

The Atom of Delight | [ornament] | NEIL M. GUNN |
[space] | FABER AND FABER LIMITED | 24 Russell Square |
London.

Collation:- [A]$^8$, B - I$^8$, NO J, K - T$^8$, 152 Leaves

p [1] THE ATOM OF DELIGHT; p [2] By the Same Author;
p[3] TITLE-PAGE; p [4] [ital] Publishers and Printers
notices: First published in MCMLVI; p 5 - 6 Contents;
p 7 - 304 Text.  5" x 7$^1$/$_2$".  BOUND IN PLUM CLOTH;
Spine stamped in Gold: THE | ATOM | OF | DELIGHT |
[ornament] | NEIL | GUNN | [space] | FABER

GUNN's  Autobiographical  work;  The  themes  are

continued in a series of articles which appeared in "The Saltire Review" between 1958 and 1961 and in "Point" in 1968 - 69

Extracts also appeared in the Glasgow Herald just prior to publication as under:-

1)  Off and Away         22.9.1956   P3
2)  Trees in Church      29.9.1956   P3
3)  The Family Cow       6.10.1956   P3
4)  The Boy in London    13.10.1956  P3

The B.B.C. Programme "Talking About Landscape" produced 28.6.1959 was a conversation between Neil Gunn and George Bruce on the same themes as the Saltire/Point Articles.

An extract from the book entitled "The Boy and the Salmon" was dramatised for Radio and produced 30.5.1957.

The typescript of this book together with two copies of corrected page proofs is held at the National Library of Scotland.

This book was remaindered 21.12.59 when the entire remaining stock of 128 bound copies and 2550 sets of sheets (out of original printing of 5050) were sold to "Books for Pleasure". The unbound sheets appear then to have been bound up in Green Paper substitute with the Title etc. stamped in black as under:-

THE | ATOM | OF | DELIGHT | NEIL | GUNN | [Space] | FABER.


A128                    (A73, A123, A129)
        PRESENTS FOR THEIR WIVES | UNPUBLISHED
            From Address                1950 - 1960

Typescript held at the National Library of Scotland. Unusually this is a story of Irish Tinkers, a subject more to the taste of GUNN's close friend Maurice Walsh. There are however close similarities to "The Old Man" and indeed a patriarchal figure again appears. The method employed in returning value for items "Borrowed" has similarities to a scene in "Bloodhunt".

A129            (A73, A128, B7, B12)
            THE PRIMROSE PATH | UNPUBLISHED
            From Address                1950 - 1960
Typescript held at the National Library of Scotland. Another Story of Irish Tinkers like "Presents For Their Wives" and "The Old Man". In this episode the old man talks of tradition with a seeker after old lore, as in "Old Music". His granddaughter Rosie, seen as the embodiment of the old spirit, is the collector of primroses destined to be a bridal bouquet.

A130    (A96,A110,A112,A119,B21,E9,E10,E33,E71)
            THE TERRIBLE ALLY | UNPUBLISHED
            From Address                1950 - 1960
Typescript held at the National Library of Scotland. The love interest in this story and the exciting voyage in an open rowing boat is virtually the same as in "The Face in the Pool" and "The Silver Bough". However these similarities are used as background to a war-time story reminiscent to some extent of parts

or "The Lost Chart" and "Sun and Moon".  He no doubt
drew on his own experiences as a coast watcher on the
West Coast of Scotland.

A131

### WHEN HALF-WAY IS ALL THE WAY | UNPUBLISHED

From Address                    1950 - 1960

Typescript held at the National Library of Scotland.
The story of three young people in a Highland
environment who are fast friends.  In adolescence the
two young men feel an attraction for the third
member, a young lady.  The boys indulge in some deer
poaching which due to over-eagerness to impress has
tragic results when one is accidentally shot by the
other.  The survivor, whilst cleared of blame, feels
he cannot remain at home and prepares to emigrate.
The girl however realising her involvement, meets the
boy in Glasgow prior to his departure, and accepts a
share in the responsibility.  By meeting half-way
their true feelings for each other become apparent.

A132                    (A56)

### JOE AND THE MONSTER | UNPUBLISHED

Typescript held at the National Library of Scotland.
This story is to all intents and purposes a
re-telling of "George and the Dragon" with an
American Newsman as hero.

A133                    (A113)

### THE ROARING GAME | UNPUBLISHED

Typescript held at the National Library of Scotland. This is little more than a dramatised description of the game of curling. It has similarities to, and the same title as an essay in "Highland Pack".

B

PLAYS DRAMATISATIONS & FILM SCRIPTS

THE HAWK'S FEATHER | THE SCOTS MAGAZINE | DUNDEE

VOL 11    NO 5    PP 328 - 340                AUGUST 1929

A one Act Play, a typescript of which is held at the
National Library of Scotland.

An allegorical play indicating, through the medium
of the supernatural, the continuing disintegration,
from the '45 to the present, of Gaelic Culture at
the hands of the English although with a change of
emphasis from military to financial prowess.  One of
his better plays.

The play was broadcast by the B.B.C. from Aberdeen
24.9.1929 performed by the Aberdeen Radio Players.
Duration 30 minutes.


B2          (A23, A24, A40, A117, A119, B23)

                THE ANCIENT FIRE | UNPUBLISHED

This Three Act Play was performed by the Scottish
National Players for Five performances commencing on
the 8th October 1929.

Typescript held at the National Library of Scotland
- Two of One version plus One of a variant.

An ambitious work concerning an urban shop owner who
goes back to his primeval homeland for a poaching
holiday.    The "pull" of one's roots and the
artificiality of modern city life are shown.   This
aspect was to be a recurrent theme throughout GUNN's
work.

There are close similarities between this work and
the contemporary serialised novel "Poaching at

Grianan" and the later play "Beyond The Cage" is obviously developed from this work.

CAST OF GLASGOW PRODUCTION:-

| | | |
|---|---|---|
| Lachie MacDonald | - | Chas. Brookes |
| Isaac Gordon | - | Tom Maley |
| Mrs. Geddes | - | Miss Anne Rae |
| Constable | - | Archibald Henderson |
| Helen MacDonald | - | Miss Meg Buchannan |
| MacDonald of Corrie | - | H.C. Stark |
| Mrs. MacLennan | - | Miss Catherine Fletcher |
| Iosbail MacDonald of | | |
| Corrie | - | Miss Grace McChlery |
| Tim Murphy | - | James Anderson |
| Jack Munro | - | Alan Mackill |
| Mrs. Reilley | - | Miss Heston Paton Brown |
| Angus Ross | - | James Gibson |
| Denver | - | Moultrie Kelsall |

B3

GLENDARUEL | THE SCOTS MAGAZINE | DUNDEE

VOL 12   NO 3   PP 177 - 187                    DECEMBER 1929

A One Act Play, A typescript of which is held at the National Library of Scotland.

Written under the pseudonym of Dane McNeil.

Three Journalists in a Glasgow Public House discuss a murder which has taken place in the vicinity. Into the discussion is woven a commentary on the state of Gaeldom and the differing outlook of Highland and Lowland Scots.

This Play was offered to the B.B.C. 17.5.34 but was

not taken up. Their representative reporting internally:-

"This affects me in the same way as Gunn's other Plays. I feel rather ashamed and sorry that he should do it at all. The novel is his form, and he seems unable to convey his ideas clearly or make his points in dialogue. From our point of view, his plays have the additional disadvantage of depending so much on expressive gesture to convey the implied but unspoken meaning. I don't think that this play could conceivably ever be broadcast; it lacks form and rhythm; it is inarticulate, and has a saddening frustration and impotence; it is just dumb as the "Talkies" have it - laocoon Gunn struggling with the dramatic Sea Serpent."

B4

### TARTAN | UNPUBLISHED

25TH MAY 1930

In the National Library of Scotland there are pages of typescript and manuscript relating to a Three Act Play of the above title. From accompanying notes it seems this was performed, probably in a school, college or university, on or around the above date. It seems probable that GUNN either wrote this or collaborated in its writing.

The Play, which calls for a knowledge of traditional Gaelic songs and prayers, is set at the time of the '45 and appears to have covered the making, wearing ana subsequent banning of the Tartan.

B5      (A24, A33, A34, A51, A107, E4, E11)

   BACK HOME | W. WILSON & CO. (GLASGOW) LTD | GLASGOW |

                1932

First Edition:-

Back Home | A PLAY IN ONE ACT | BY NEIL M. GUNN |

[Space] | WALTER WILSON & CO.(GLASGOW) LTD | JAMAICA

STREET | GLASGOW | 1932

Collation:-[A]$^8$, B$^8$, 16 Leaves.

Stiff Paper Cover, Pasted to pp [1] and [32], with

Cover Title: SCOTTISH NATIONAL PLAYS SERIES NO 9 |

[cut] | Back Home | by Neil M. Gunn | [At    Bottom,    to

The Left] ONE SHILLING NET.

p [2] This Series of Plays is published | under    the

auspices of the Saint | Andrew   Society  (Glasgow);  p

[3] SCOTTISH  NATIONAL  PLAYS  SERIES  No  9; p [4]

Copyright notice, note on performing rights and fee,

printers notice; p [5] Title Page; p [6] Publishers

notice; p [7] NOTE [from the Publishers]: p [8]

CHARACTERS  p  [9]  10  -  26  text;  p  [27]  -  [29]

publisher's advertisements; p [30] [31] blank.  On

back Cover: [cut] BONE & HULLEY | 25  Dundas  Street,

Glasgow [in rectangular frame of dots]

This play was later collected in:-

THE   BEST   ONE-ACT   PLAYS   OF  1931,  Selected  by

J.W. MARRIOTT | GEORGE G. HARRAP & CO. LTD | LONDON |

1932 PP 271 - 285

Broadcast with slight textual variations 16.8.1937.

On the Scottish Regional Programme of the B.B.C.

PRODUCER - ANDREW STEWART, DURATION 25 MINS. TYPESCRIPT HELD AT B.B.C. GLASGOW.

Gaelic version Broadcast by B.B.C. under Title "Tilleadh Dhachaidh" on Scottish Home Service 13.3.47.

PRODUCER HUGH MACPHEE. NO SCRIPT

The first One Act Play to see National Publication. The basic theme was explored in prose in the Scots Magazine (March 1928) under Title "The Man Who Came Back". Deals with the failure attributed to persons who choose to return from "better" posts in cities to their native land and employment. The Novel "The Drinking Well" further expands.

B6                         (A65, B8)

CHOOSING A PLAY : A COMEDY OF COMMUNITY DRAMA

THE SCOTS MAGAZINE | DUNDEE

VOL 23   NO 2   PP 99 - 112                    MAY 1935

This Play was later collected in:-

"SCOTTISH ONE ACT PLAYS" Ed. J.M. Reid | THE PORPOISE PRESS | 1935 | PP 117 - 140

Then issued as an individual One Act Play by

THE PORPOISE PRESS | EDINBURGH | 24.2.1938

A humorous discussion amongst a Drama Society trying to decide on a play for production. Under the surface the play becomes a commentary on the state of Scotland. In concept this work is similar to "Raw Material". It was also offered to the B.B.C. 6.11.1936, but there is no record of it having been produced.

It is however reported to have been presented in
Inverness on the stage.

B7                    (A58, A129, B12, E3)
          OLD MUSIC | THE SCOTS MAGAZINE | DUNDEE
VOL 23   NO 4   PP 254 - 266                    JULY 1935
Subsequently broadcast by the B.B.C. - Production
19.6.36 - Typescript held at B.B.C.
PRODUCER  ANDREW STEWART.  DURATION 25 MINS.
Scottish Regional Programme.
Later issued as an individual One Act Play by NELSON
(NELSONS PLAYS FOR AMATEURS NO 2) | LONDON 1939  - See
Separate Entry.
This play was later collected in:-
NORTH LIGHT ED. WINIFRED BANNISTER | WILLIAM   MACLELLAN
| GLASGOW | 1947 | PP 44 - 61
An Old Lady living in a crofting community is grief
stricken as she sees her grandson, embodying the
future of the area, emigrate.  As she croons a Gaelic
lament her home is invaded by English Folk, taking
advantage of Highland hospitality, collecting old
songs on tape for posterity and press her, in her
distress, to sing.


B8                    (A65, B6)
     CHOOSING A PLAY | THE PORPOISE PRESS | EDINBURGH
                              24th FEBRUARY 1938
     (THE EDITION IS NOT DATED BUT THE DATE HAS
        BEEN SUPPLIED BY THE PUBLISHERS)

95

First Separate Edition:-

CHOOSING A PLAY | [ital] A COMEDY OF COMMUNITY DRAMA |
(FOR J.M.) | by | NEIL M̊. GUNN | [ital] CHARACTERS |
FLORA AND DON, players | A PRODUCER | MOTHER AND SON |
[Space] | [in brackets] Permission to produce this
play should be obtained from | Messrs. FABER AND FABER
LTD. 24 Russell Square | London, W.C.1.

Collation:-[A]$^8$, I$^8$, 16 Leaves.

2 Blank leaves; Title Page; Reverse Blank; Text p 119
- 140; 2 Blank leaves.

Bound with paper wrapper, pasted to spine and flapped
round the first and last leaves, in Orange printed in
Black.

On front cover:-

NEIL M. GUNN | [line] | CHOOSING | A PLAY | [ital] A
comedy | [ital] of Community Drama | [line] | The
Porpoise Press.

On front flap, in bottom R.H. corner 1s. | Net.

On back flap, at top - Advertisement for the Porpoise
Press.

On back cover - THE FABER LIBRARY - List of 39 Vols.

This is a reissue of pp 117 - 140 of "Scotish One Act
Plays" ed. John MacNair Reid | THE PORPOISE PRESS |
EDINBURGH | 1935

The Play first appeared in:-

THE SCOTS MAGAZINE | DUNDEE | VOL 23   NO 2 | PP 99 - 112
| MAY 1935

SEE THAT ENTRY FOR NOTES.


B9

HAIL, CALEDONIAN! | THE SCOTS MAGAZINE | DUNDEE
VOL 29   NO 2   PP 113 - 122                    MAY 1938
A One Act Play on the Caledonian Electricity Power
Bill and its non adoption on environmental grounds.
His conclusion is that he believes this decision to
be counter to the long term interest of the Highlands
and its people.


B10                    (A62, B13)

        NET RESULTS | THE SCOTS MAGAZINE | DUNDEE
VOL 29   NO 4   PP 289 - 303                    JULY 1938
Later issued as an individual One Act Play by NELSON
(NELSON'S PLAYS FOR AMATEURS NO 11) | LONDON 1939
A bitter little play about the plight of the herring
fisheries of the North East.  With the fall off in
catches  and  the  poorer  prices  difficulties  were
experienced with meeting repayments on the bank loan
for the purchase of their boat.


B11

    THE BRIDGE BUILDER | THE SCOTS MAGAZINE | DUNDEE
VOL 32   NO 2   PP 101 - 116                NOVEMBER 1939
A One Act Play based on the difficulties encountered
by Telford in his construction of the Caledonian
Canal.  GUNN said of this work:- "The moral is that
of the engineer who will go on building his bridges
though wars should blow then sky-high"


B12                (A58, A129, B7, E3)

        OLD MUSIC | NELSON | LONDON | 1939

NO EXACT DATE OF PUBLICATION CAN BE GIVEN

BY PUBLISHERS BUT DATE OF AGREEMENT 26.9.39

<u>First Edition</u>:-

OLD MUSIC | [Space] | by | NEIL M. GUNN | [Space] | THOMAS
NELSON AND SONS LTD | LONDON EDINBURGH PARIS MELBOURNE
| TORONTO AND NEW YORK

<u>Collation</u>:-[A]$^{14}$, 14 Leaves

p [1] NELSON'S PLAYS FOR AMATEURS | General    Editor:
Nora Ratcliff, M.A. | [ornament] | [space] | OLD MUSIC |
[space] | No 2; p [2] Copyright: Neil M. Gunn, 1939;
p [3] Title Page; p [4] CHARACTERS; p 5 - 25 Text; p
[26] ACTING NOTES; p [27] PRINTED IN GREAT BRITAIN AT
| THE PRESS OF THE PUBLISHERS; p [28] Blank

$5^1/_8$" x $7^1/_4$". Stiff paper Cover, with Cover Title:
OLD MUSIC | by | NEIL M. GUNN | NELSON'S    PLAYS    FOR
AMATEURS 1/= Net.

Later Collected in:-

NORTH LIGHT, ED. WINIFRED BANNISTER | WILLIAM
MACLELLAN | GLASGOW | 1947 | PP 44 - 61

The Play first appeared in THE SCOTS MAGAZINE | DUNDEE
| VOL 23   NO 4 | PP 254 - 266 | JULY 1935

SEE ENTRY UNDER THAT DATE FOR DETAILS.


B13                      (A62, B10)

NET RESULTS | NELSON | LONDON | 1939

NO EXACT DATE OF PUBLICATION CAN BE GIVEN BY

PUBLISHERS BUT DATE OF AGREEMENT 26.9.39

<u>First Edition</u>:-

NET RESULTS | [space] | by | NEIL M. GUNN | [space] |
THOMAS NELSON AND SONS LTD | LONDON    EDINBURGH    PARIS

MELBOURNE | TORONTO AND NEW YORK

<u>Collation</u>:-[A]$^{16}$.  16 Leaves

p [1] NELSONS PLAYS FOR AMATEURS | General      Editor:
Nora Ratcliff, M.A. | [ornament] | [space] | NET  RESULTS
| [space] | No 11; p [2] Copyright Notices; p [3] Title
Page; p [4] CHARACTERS; p 5 - 29 Text; p 30 STAGE
PLAN; p 31 ACTING NOTES; p [32] PRINTED IN GREAT
BRITAIN AT | THE PRESS OF THE PUBLISHERS.

$5^1/_8$" x $7^1/_4$".  Stiff Paper Cover, with Cover Title:
NET | RESULTS | by | NEIL M. GUNN | NELSON'S  PLAYS  FOR
AMATEURS 1/= net.

This Play was first published in:-

THE SCOTS MAGAZINE | DUNDEE | VOL 29 NO 4 | PP 289 - 303
| JULY 1938

SEE THAT ENTRY FOR COMMENT.


B14     (A40, A74, A80, A117, B29, D212, E44)

SECOND SIGHT | UNPUBLISHED

This Three Act Play was never, to the best of my
knowledge, produced.  It was offered to the B.B.C.
for Broadcasting but was declined.  From an
accompanying letter to the B.B.C. (11.1.1956) it
transpires that the novel which bears the same name
and follows the same plot was developed from this
play.  GUNN writes "I once wrote a play on Second
Sight, and not knowing what to do with it I turned it
into a Novel".

The Play was also unsuccessfully offered to THE
WILSON BARRETT LTD COMPANY who produced "BEYOND THE
CAGE"

A typescript bearing his Cannich address, presumably prepared in 1956 at the time of the approach to the B.B.C. is held at the National Library of Scotland. The Novel was published 11.4.1940.


B15                    (A113, D74, E5)

        THE LAND WE DEFEND - THE WESTERN HIGHLANDS
        AND ISLANDS OF SCOTLAND | B.B.C. PRODUCTION
                PRODUCER        -       MOULTRIE R. KELSALL
                PROGRAMME       -       SCOTTISH HOME SERVICE
                DURATION        -       30 MINUTES
                DATE            -       30TH AUGUST 1940

Typescripts held at the B.B.C. Glasgow and The National Library of Scotland.

This piece was written especially for Radio and was intended to highlight the homeland; its countryside, people and occupations. It was written in Play form with the various regions and the sea being personified. It falls into three parts; the first an argument between the regions on their respective attractions, the second recounts the hazardous sea journey involved in taking sheep to summer grazing on rocky islets and the third is a conversation between servicemen on leave highlighting what they look forward to doing.

B16                    (B17, E6)

            LEWIS TODAY | B.B.C. PRODUCTION
                PRODUCER        -       MOULTRIE R. KELSALL
                PROGRAMME       -       SCOTTISH HOME SERVICE
                DURATION        -       30 MINUTES

DATE          -     10TH DECEMBER 1941

Typescripts are held at the B.B.C. Script Library (Plays) London, B.B.C. Glasgow and The National Library of Scotland who also held scripts entitled "Drama in Lewis" and "Lewis in War Time". These are both earlier versions of the same text.

This specially commissioned piece commented on the effect of the war on the Islanders of Lewis and was produced in Play form.

The programme was well received generally and received favourable press comment.


B17                    (B16, E6)

LEWIS TODAY | STORNOWAY GAZETTE AND WEST
COAST ADVERTISER | STORNOWAY

VOL 26  NO 1300  P 2             2ND JANUARY 1942
VOL 26  NO 1301  P 2             9TH JANUARY 1942
VOL 26  NO 1302  P 2            16TH JANUARY 1942

Three extracts from the B.B.C. Broadcast of the same title 10.12.1941.


B18                    (E7)

HIGHLAND PROSPECT | B.B.C. PRODUCTION

PRODUCER      -     MOULTRIE R. KELSALL

PROGRAMME     -     SCOTTISH HOME SERVICE

DURATION      -     40 MINUTES

DATE          -     10TH OCTOBER 1942

Typescripts are held at the B.B.C. Script Library (Plays) London, B.B.C. Glasgow and The National Library of Scotland who also hold a script entitled

"Tne Northern Highlands Today". This is an earlier version of the same text.

In Play form this consists of discussions amongst Highland P.o.W's en route to a new camp in Bavaria. They talk of their Homeland with particular reference to economic/social conditions. Use is made of "flash backs" to conversations in their homes.


B19

### BLUE PRINT FOR THE HIGHLANDS | UNPUBLISHED
### FILM SCRIPT

17TH MAY 1943

The film was produced by "ROTHA FILMS" - PAUL ROTHA PRODUCTIONS LTD and a copy of the commentary is held at the National Library of Scotland.

The film deals with possible plans for post war development in the Highlands.


B20                    (A31, A76, E8)

### THE BLACK WOOLLEN GLOVES | B.B.C. PRODUCTION

|  |  |  |
|---|---|---|
| PRODUCER | - | MOULTRIE R. KELSALL |
| PROGRAMME | - | SCOTTISH HOME SERVICE |
| DURATION | - | 30 MINUTES |
| DATE | - | 8TH FEBRUARY 1944 |

Typescripts held at the B.B.C. Script Library (Plays) London, B.B.C. Glasgow and the National Library of Scotland.

A dramatisation by GUNN of his short story of the same name which appeared in the SCOTS MAGAZINE in

January 1928.

This was perhaps not too well received - in the B.B.C. file is a note from the producer relating to the later "Sun and Moon" in which he states "It's a lot better than "The Black Woollen Gloves" (it would need to be).

B21      (A96, A112, A130, E9, E10, E33, E71)

       SUN AND MOON | B.B.C. PRODUCTION

| | | |
|---|---|---|
| PRODUCER | - | MOULTRIE R. KELSALL |
| PROGRAMME | - | SCOTTISH HOME SERVICE |
| DURATION | - | 30 MINUTES |
| DATE | - | 1ST JUNE 1944 |
| | | REPEATED 6TH FEB.1947 |

NEW PRODUCTION

| | | |
|---|---|---|
| PRODUCER | - | FINLAY J. MACDONALD |
| PROGRAMME | - | SCOTTISH HOME SERVICE |
| DURATION | - | 35 MINUTES |
| DATE | - | 28TH MARCH 1956 |
| | | REPEATED 29TH JUNE |
| | | 1960 (40 MINS) |

Typescript held at the B.B.C. Script Library (Plays) London, B.B.C. Glasgow and the National Library of Scotland.

A dramatisation by GUNN of his short story of the same name which appeared in the SCOTS MAGAZINE in November 1942.

B22          (A113, D140)

    OLD HIGHLAND BALLET | UNPUBLISHED SCRIPT

This Play script was produced with a view to it being peformed by the B.B.C. and can be dated from correspondence. It was however never performed.

The Play related to the folk dances of the old Highland communities which have been largely lost.

Typescript held at The National Library of Scotland.

A Chapter of "Highland Pack" entitled "Dancing in the Highlands" followed the same theme.

B23        (A23, A24, A40, A117, A119, B2)

### BEYOND THE CAGE

This Three Act Play was produced by the WILSON BARRETT COMPANY for the Edinburgh Festival of 1952 (25th - 30th August) but had a preview at the Alhambra Theatre Glasgow on the 18th August 1952.

Typescript held at The National Library of Scotland.

The plot of this Play follows closely that of "The Ancient Fire" from which it has been developed - see notes against that entry.

A further typescript is held at The National Library of Scotland, originally entitled "A Poaching Holiday", which has been altered to read "Beyond The Cage". This is not the same text as the Play produced but is an interim stage between "The Ancient Fire" and the final production.

Cast of Edinburgh Festival Production:-

| | |
|---|---|
| Rory MacDonald | - Wilfred Carter |
| Angus Ross | - Frank Raymond |
| Isaac Drobny | - John Schlesinger |

| | | |
|---|---|---|
| Tim Murphy | – | Leon Sinden |
| Mrs. Geddes | – | Edith MacArthur |
| Mrs. Paterson | – | Freda Fergusson |
| Helen MacDonald | – | Ruth Porcher |
| The Policeman | – | Walter Carr |
| The MacDonald of Corriemore | – | Stuart Black |
| Mrs. MacLennan | – | Molly Francis |
| The Voice of young Helen | – | Caroline Raitt |

B24         (A59, D198, E25)

HERITAGE NO. 18 "THE HIGHLAND CLEARANCES" |

B.B.C. PRODUCTION

| | | |
|---|---|---|
| PRODUCER | – | ROBIN RICHARDSON |
| PROGRAMME | – | SCOTTISH HOME SERVICE |
| DURATION | – | 60 MINUTES |
| DATE | – | 12TH DECEMBER 1954 |

Typescripts held at the B.B.C. Glasgow and The National Library of Scotland.

A reflection on the clearances presented in dramatic form as a conversation.

An article by GUNN appeared in the Radio Times 10.12.1954 entitled "The Tragedy of the Highland Clearances".

B25          (A63)

HERITAGE NO. 23 "WHISKY" | B.B.C. PRODUCTION

| | | |
|---|---|---|
| PRODUCER | – | ROBIN RICHARDSON |
| PROGRAMME | – | SCOTTISH HOME SERVICE |
| DURATION | – | 60 MINUTES |
| DATE | – | 30TH DECEMBER 1954 |

Typescripts held at the B.B.C. Edinburgh and The National Library of Scotland.

A study into the history and making of Scotland's National Drink told in a dramatic format.

B26                    (E34)

    THE SEA TO THE ISLES | B.B.C. PRODUCTION

| | | |
|---|---|---|
| PRODUCER | - | ROBIN RICHARDSON |
| PROGRAMME | - | SCOTTISH HOME SERVICE |
| DURATION | - | 45 MINUTES |
| DATE | - | 9TH AUGUST 1956 |

Typescripts held at the B.B.C. Glasgow and The National Library of Scotland.

A description of the Hebrides and their history seen from the sea - that connecting highway.  The work is dramatised as a conversation.

An article about this broadcast appeared in the Radio Times (Scottish Edition) | London | Vol  132  No 1708 | P 9 | 3.8.1956  entitled  "The  Magic  of  the Western Isles".

B27                    (A127, E41)

    THE BOY AND THE SALMON | B.B.C. PRODUCTION

| | | |
|---|---|---|
| PRODUCER | - | FINLAY J. MACDONALD |
| PROGRAMME | - | SCOTTISH HOME SERVICE |
| DURATION | - | 60 MINUTES |
| DATE | - | 30TH MAY 1957 |

Typescripts held at the B.B.C. Script Library (Plays) London and the National Library of Scotland.

A dramatised extract from "The Atom of Delight" in

which the boy GUNN catches a large salmon with his
bare hands.

An article about this broadcast entitled:- "The Boy
and the Salmon" appeared in the Radio Times
(Scottish Edition) | London | Vol 135 | No 1750 | P 6 |
24.5.1957


B28                    (E43)

  "THIS IS MY COUNTRY" - LIVING IN THE HIGHLANDS I
  "GOOD NEWS COMES TO THE GLEN" | B.B.C. PRODUCTION
      PROGRAMME   -  SCOTTISH HOME SERVICE (SCHOOLS)
      DURATION    -  20 MINUTES
      DATE        -  1ST NOVEMBER 1957
      PRODUCER    -  TOM ALLEN
Typescripts held at the B.B.C. Edinburgh and The
National Library of Scotland.

The story of the "Crofters' Charter" of 1886 told in
dramatic form as a conversation.


B29        (A74, A80, B14, D212, E44)

  "THIS IS MY COUNTRY" - LIVING IN THE HIGHLANDS II
        "DEER STALKING" | B.B.C. PRODUCTION
      PROGRAMME   -  SCOTTISH HOME SERVICE (SCHOOLS)
      DURATION    -  20 MINUTES
      DATE        -  8TH NOVEMBER 1957
      PRODUCER    -  TOM ALLEN
Typescripts held at the B.B.C. Edinburgh and The
National Library of Scotland.

A dramatised exposition of the sport.

B30 (E45)

"THIS IS MY COUNTRY" - LIVING IN THE HIGHLANDS III

"ALL IN A LIFETIME" | B.B.C. PRODUCTION

PROGRAMME    - SCOTTISH HOME SERVICE (SCHOOLS)

DURATION     - 20 MINUTES

DATE         - 15TH NOVEMBER 1957

PRODUCER     - TOM ALLEN

Typescripts held at the B.B.C. Edinburgh and The National Library of Scotland.

In this play the changes seen within one generation in the Highland way of life are highlighted.

B31 (A63)

THE WATER OF LIFE | UNPUBLISHED    FILM    SCRIPT

This film script was produced for Associated British Pictures Ltd. but was never proceeded with. The script bears only the name of Neil M. GUNN but, from correspondence between GUNN and A.B.P. Ltd., it is clear that Maurice Walsh collaborated. His style is evident in some parts of the work.

There is a typescript of this work at The National Library of Scotland.

The whole is a romantic thriller centred on Highland whisky production both official and otherwise. There are some superficial likenesses to "The Poaching at Grianan", "The Ancient Fire" and "Beyond The Cage". The work also includes much of the subject matter of the B.B.C. Production "Whisky" and the smuggling scene from "The Well at the Worlds End".

108

Correspondence dates the work April 1958.

B32                    (A63)

## THE STORY OF TORMORE | UNPUBLISHED COMMENTARY
### FOR A FILM

24TH NOVEMBER 1960

The film was produced by The Films of Scotland
Committee for Long John Whisky and a typescript is
held at the National Library of Scotland.

The date quoted is that which appears on the script
although there is a story outline/shooting script
attached dated 1958.

The film relates to the building of a new Whisky
Distillery and attendant workers village at Tormore,
Speyside.  The official opening was 7.10.1960 and
the programme contained "The Long John Story" also
by GUNN.

The central character Donald pays visits also to
local fishing, deer stalking and highland games to
give a picture of Highland traditions.

Many of the comments regarding distilling follow
patterns used elsewhere in GUNN'S work, principally
"Whisky and Scotland".

Long John needed the assistance of someone eminent
in Scottish letters who also had a knowledge of
distilling.   GUNN was employed by them as a
consultant on Scottish matters for some years during
which time this film was made.

John Mackie who worked for the company recalls
taking Neil to sample the water of the Burn which

supplies the distillery before building commenced. After taking one sip he said in his gentle voice "You cannot fail to get good whisky from this water."

B33

OVER THE SEA TO SKYE | UNPUBLISHED FILM SCRIPT

1962

A film of this title was made by Anvil Films (Scotland) Ltd. which correspondence dates 1962. On deposit with the National Library of Scotland is an "Article" with the same title which I suspect is probably the commentary for this film.

At around the same time it is believed that the same Company made a film called "Highland Folk Museum" but I have been unable to obtain further details.

B34

INVERNESS, PIPE BANDS IN ACTION | UNPUBLISHED

25TH JUNE 1966

Typescript held at the National Library of Scotland. This piece looks like part of something intended for Radio T.V., or Films. The "Pipe Bands in Action" seems to be an instruction for musical accompaniment. It is followed by Iona (Iona Boat Song). It may have been commentary on a film of the World Pipe Band Contest and the gathering of the clans on 25th June 1966 which is referred to in the text.

MAJORCA: IDEA FOR A FILM | UNPUBLISHED

27TH MARCH 1969

A typescript which accompanied a letter to Mr. Clark of Associated British Picture Corporation set out some ideas for a film set in Majorca. There is no evidence that this idea was proceeded with.

Typescript held at The National Library of Scotland.

C

VERSE

C1                          (F1)

"TOAST" | THE APPLE TREE | LONDON

VOL 1   NO 1   P 1                          MAY 1918

Poem to commemorate the first issue of the House
Journal of the Aspirants Fellowship.

Was signed NIAL GUINNE (The Gaelic Form of his Name)

This has been identified as GUNN's first appearance
in print.


C2

    LA MADELEINE | THE SCOTTISH CHAPBOOK | MONTROSE

VOL 1   NO 7   P 200                        FEB. 1923

Subtitled (From a Painting by Henner)


C3

    TO A REDBREAST | THE SCOTTISH CHAPBOOK | MONTROSE

VOL 1   NO 10   P 273                       MAY 1923


C4

    TO MY GRAMOPHONE | THE SCOTTISH CHAPBOOK | MONTROSE

VOL 1   NO 11   P 323                       JUNE 1923


C5                     (A43, A98, C9)

    O SUN | THE SCOTTISH CHAPBOOK | MONTROSE

VOL 1   NO 12   P 329                    23RD JULY 1923


C6

    THE FIRST TRUMP | THE SCOTS MAGAZINE | DUNDEE

VOL 9   NO 4   P 261                        JULY 1928

Written under the Pseudonym Dane McNeil.

C7

SUB ROSA | THE SCOTS MAGAZINE | DUNDEE

VOL 10　　NO 3　　P 172　　　　　　　　　　DECEMBER 1928


C8

TO W.H. HUDSON | THE SCOTS MAGAZINE | DUNDEE

VOL 11　　NO 2　　P 102　　　　　　　　　　　　MAY 1929


C9　　　　　　　(A43, A98, A113, C5)

THE SERPENT | THE MODERN SCOT | DUNDEE

VOL 1　　NO 1　　P 36　　　　　　　　　　　SPRING 1930

The scene evoked was utilised in the novel of the
Same Name (Faber & Faber 1943) and bears
similarities to the Poem "O Sun".

This poem was reprinted as part of the Chapter "The
Frightened Worm" in the Book:-

HIGHLAND PACK | FABER & FABER | 18th　NOVEMBER　1949

P 27


C10　　　　　　　　　　(A28)

TO ONE WHO LISTENED | FROM "OUR SINGER AND HER SONGS"

TO MARJORY KENNEDY-FRASER Mus.Doc.(Edin),C.B.E.　AND

HER SONGS OF THE HEBRIDES OUR CORDIAL TRIBUTES |

PATRICK GEDDES AND COLLEAGUES | EDINBURGH | 1930

P 27

A collection of Tributes at a time when Mrs.
Kennedy-Fraser was ill.

The date on one letter suggests Publication in
Oct. 1930.

C11

VITALITY | THE SCOTS MAGAZINE | DUNDEE

VOL 16    NO 2 Page 122                    NOVEMBER 1931

D

**ARTICLES IN NEWSPAPERS AND PERIODICALS**

D1

AT THE PEATS | CHAMBERS'S JOURNAL | EDINBURGH

SEVENTH SERIES VOL 13   NO 650   PP 369 - 371

12TH MAY 1923


D2

ENGLISH SOLDIERS IN CAITHNESS |

THE GLASGOW HERALD | GLASGOW

141ST YEAR   NO 156   P 4            30TH JUNE 1923

This piece was anonymous in the newspaper but a
cutting retained with GUNN's papers deposited with
the National Library of Scotland has been initialled
in ink and is clearly therefore written by him.


D3                        (D250)

FALCONRY : A DAY WITH THE HAWKS | CHAMBERS'S JOURNAL

EDINBURGH | SEVENTH SERIES VOL 14 NO 690

PP 180 - 184                16TH FEBRUARY 1924


D4

WHITE FISHING ON THE CAITHNESS COAST |

CHAMBERS'S JOURNAL | EDINBURGH | SEVENTH SERIES

VOL 14   NO 723   PP 708 - 710        4TH OCTOBER 1924


D5

JOHN O'GROATS | CHAMBERS'S JOURNAL | EDINBURGH

SEVENTH SERIES   VOL 15   NO 737   PP 81 - 83

10TH JANUARY 1925


D6

A NORTHERN NIGHT | CHAMBERS'S JOURNAL | EDINBURGH

SEVENTH SERIES   VOL 16   NO 828   PP 716 - 717

9TH OCTOBER 1926


D7

DEFENSIO SCOTORUM - A REPLY TO W.S. MORRISON

MARCH 1928 | THE SCOTS MAGAZINE | DUNDEE

VOL 9   NO 1   PP 51 - 58                    APRIL 1928

Written under the Pseudonym Dane McNeil


This article was in reply to:-

DEFENSIO SCOTORUM - A REPLY TO A NATION'S CRITICS BY

W.S. MORRISON | THE SCOTS MAGAZINE | DUNDEE

VOL 8   NO 6   PP 401 - 410                  MARCH 1928


D8

THE HIDDEN HEART | THE SCOTS MAGAZINE | DUNDEE

VOL 9   NO 5   PP 331 - 335                 AUGUST 1928

Written under the Pseudonym Dane McNeil.


D9

THE NEW VITALITY IN SCOTTISH LITERATURE

EVIDENCES OF THE RENAISSANCE : I FEMININE |

DAILY RECORD | GLASGOW

No 25585   P5                          23RD JANUARY 1929

An article on the work of Marian Angus.


D10

MY BEST DAYS FISHING | THE SCOTS MAGAZINE | DUNDEE

VOL 10   NO 4   PP 260 - 261               JANUARY 1929

118

Written under the Pseudonym of Dane McNeil.

D11                    (D213, D217, E42)

SCOTLAND'S GREATEST POET OF TO-DAY

EVIDENCES OF THE RENAISSANCE : 2 - THE MASCULINE |

DAILY RECORD | GLASGOW

NO 25597   P 18                    6TH FEBRUARY 1929

An article on Hugh MacDiarmid.


D12

CABBAGES, HONEY AND THE KAILYARD |

THE SCOTS OBSERVER | GLASGOW

VOL 3  NO 125  P 8                16TH FEBRUARY 1929


D13

THE SCOTTISH LITERARY RENAISSANCE MOVEMENT |

WICK MERCANTILE DEBATING SOCIETY MAGAZINE | WICK

VOL 1  NO 1  PP 16 - 17                    APRIL 1929

Only one copy, in private hands, of this magazine
has been traced. There was, so far as can be
ascertained only one publication - No.1 was first
and last. The magazine is described as being 7.3" x
9.7" with a stiff pink paper cover. There are 15
pages of adverts, a page with details of the
officers and committee, a portrait of the Hon.
President and twenty pages of text with two columns
to the page.

This article was reprinted in THE SCOTTISH LITERARY
JOURNAL | ABERDEEN

VOL 4   NO 2   PP 58 - 61         DECEMBER 1977

D14                     (D16)

PADRAIC PEARSE | THE SCOTS INDEPENDENT | GLASGOW

Part    I)  'The Man Called Pearse'    Vol IV No 1

PP 9 - 10                              NOVEMBER 1929

Part II)  'Poems, Plays and Stories'   Vol IV No 2

P 21                                   DECEMBER 1929

Written    under    the    Pseudonym    of    Dane    McNeil


D15

CHANTICLEER | DOGS | NEW FORMS

I  have  been  unable  to  positively  identify  these
articles but, from the format, I am reasonably sure
they  appeared  in  the  GLASGOW  HERALD  during  the
Nineteen Twenties.


D16                     (D14)

PADRAIC PEARSE | THE SCOTS INDEPENDENT | GLASGOW

Part III)  'The Sovereign People'   Vol IV No 3 P 33
                                       JANUARY   1930

Written    under    the    Pseudonym    of    Dane    McNeil


D17                     (D18)

THE HIGHLAND CRISIS - A HIDDEN LIFE NOW
DEMANDS EXPRESSION I THE CROFTERS HARDSHIPS
THE SCOTS OBSERVER | GLASGOW

P6                              16TH JANUARY 1930

Written under the Pseudonym of Dane McNeil.


120

D18 (D17)

THE HIGHLAND CRISIS - SCOTLAND IS ACTUALLY

A RICH COUNTRY II THE EXAMPLE OF OTHER COUNTRIES

| THE SCOTS OBSERVER | GLASGOW

P 6                                      23RD JANUARY 1930

Written under the Pseudonym of Dane McNeil.


D19

HERRING FISHING | OBSERVER | LONDON

18TH MAY 1930

This article was written by GUNN but signed "By a Special Correspondent".

A cutting of this is held with the papers lodged at the National Library of Scotland. The copy held at the Colindale Library has the same article on the reverse of the page but does not carry the above article. It would seem therefore that there was a different, presumably Northern or Scottish, Edition but I have been unable to trace a copy and cannot quote page numbers etc.


D20

NEW GOLDEN AGE FOR SCOTS LETTERS |

DAILY RECORD | GLASGOW

NO 26004  P 5                            28TH MAY 1930


D21

THE SHORES OF MORAY |

S.M.T. MAGAZINE | EDINBURGH

VOL 4 NO 6  PP 116 - 118                 JUNE 1930

D22

THE HIGHLAND EXHIBITION AT INVERNESS |

S.M.T. MAGAZINE | EDINBURGH

VOL 5   NO 2   PP 22 - 24                    AUGUST 1930


D23               (D38, D115, D168, D209)

THE DUNBEATH COAST | CAITHNESS YOUR HOME |

HERBERT SINCLAIR | LONDON

P3                                      NOVEMBER 1930

The Above article appeared in "CAITHNESS YOUR HOME"
an   anthology   Edited   and   Published   by   HERBERT
SINCLAIR.   PP  4 - 8  were  taken  up  by  accompanying
photographs.

The article was later included in the undermentioned
anthology:-

WHISPERING WINDS | RONALD THOMSON | EDINBURGH | 1975 |
PP 6 - 7.


D24

THE GAEL WILL COME AGAIN |

THE SCOTS MAGAZINE | DUNDEE

VOL 14   NO 5   PP 324 - 327            FEBRUARY 1931

Written under the Pseudonym of Dane McNeil.

A reply to "CELT AND NORSEMAN" by ALEXANDER URQUHART
- SCOTS MAGAZINE | JANUARY 1931.


D25

NATIONALISM AND INTERNATIONALISM |

THE SCOTS MAGAZINE | DUNDEE

VOL 15 NO 3 PP 185 - 188                    JUNE 1931

D26

HIGHLAND GAMES |

THE SCOTS MAGAZINE | DUNDEE

VOL 15   NO 6   PP 412 - 416            SEPTEMBER 1931


D27

AUTUMN IN THE CUILLIN |

THE SCOTS MAGAZINE | DUNDEE

VOL 16   NO 3   PP 174 - 176            DECEMBER 1931


D28

MacGILLIVRAY - SOURCES OF HIS GENIUS |

SCOTTISH ACTION | EDINBURGH

NO 2   PP 4 - 5                    31ST OCTOBER 1932

There were only two issues of "SCOTTISH ACTION" which was published with the main aim of promoting PITTENDRIGH MacGILLIVRAY'S election as rector of Edinburgh University.

The typescript of a draft of this article under the title "ELEMENTS OF NATIONALITY" is held at the National Library of Scotland.


D29

THE SCOTTISH RENASCENCE |

THE SCOTS MAGAZINE | DUNDEE

VOL 19   NO 3   PP 201 - 204                JUNE 1933

Written under the Pseudonym of Dane McNeil.

A reply to an article by G.L. RAYNE in THE SCOTS MAGAZINE Vol 19  No 2  MAY 1933.

D30

THE STRATHS AND SEA ROADS OF THE NORTH EAST |

S.M.T. MAGAZINE | EDINBURGH | VOL 11 NO 1   PP 93 - 101

JULY   1933


D31

BOY, WHAT ARE YOUR DREAMS |

B.B. BULLETIN | GLASGOW |

NO 3   P 9                                    6TH SEPTEMBER 1933

This was a special publication which ran from
4th - 11th Sept. 1933.   Commemorating the Silver
Jubilee of the Boy's Brigade Movement.

This was printed by GEORGE OUTRAM & CO. and was the
Official Publication for the Glasgow Celebrations.


D32                        (A113)

HILL SHADOWS |

THE SCOTS MAGAZINE | DUNDEE

VOL 19   NO 6   PP 430 - 434              SEPTEMBER 1933

A Nature article later used as part of "HIGHLAND PACK"


D33

THE SYMBOL OF SCOTLAND |

SCOTTISH FIELD | GLASGOW

VOL 64   NO 381   PP 165 - 166 & 168    SEPTEMBER 1934

A reply to the article "SYMBOLS GONE ASTRAY" by HUGH
MUNRO in SCOTTISH FIELD, AUGUST 1934 PP 95 - 96.


D34

124

THE INNER MAN |

SCOTLAND | GLASGOW

VOL 1   NO 6   PP 51 - 54                    SUMMER 1935

'Scotland' was the organ of The Scottish National
Development Council.


D35

FREE FISHING |

S.M.T. MAGAZINE | EDINBURGH

VOL 15   NO 4   PP 39 - 41                    OCTOBER 1935


D36

DOOM IN THE MORAY FIRTH |

THE SCOTS MAGAZINE | DUNDEE

VOL 24   NO 1   PP 24 - 27                    OCTOBER 1935

Written under the Pseudonym of Dane McNeil.


D37

PRESERVING THE SCOTTISH TONGUE |

THE SCOTS MAGAZINE | DUNDEE

VOL 24   NO 2   PP 105 - 114                    NOVEMBER 1935


D38                (D23, D115, D168, D209)

CAITHNESS AND SUTHERLAND |

FROM 'SCOTTISH COUNTRY' | WISHART BOOKS LTD |

PP 59 - 76                                        1935

One of a collection of essays by Scottish Authors on
the people and scenery of various regions of
Scotland.  Edited and with an introduction by GEORGE
SCOTT MONCRIEFF.

D39                    (A113)

WELLS AND WISHES |

THE SCOTS MAGAZINE | DUNDEE

VOL 25   NO 3   PP 195 - 199                    JUNE 1936

A  Nature  article  later  used  as  part  of  "HIGHLAND

PACK"


D40        LITERATURE: CLASS OR NATIONAL? |

OUTLOOK | EDINBURGH |

VOL 1   NO 4   PP 54 - 58                    JULY 1936

A  reply  to  an  article  by  L.  KERR  in  OUTLOOK  Vol 1

No 3   June 1936.


D41

THE GAEL DEMANDS THAT THE CROFT SURVIVES

1936

A  cutting  is  held  with  GUNN's  private  papers  at  the

National  Library  of  Scotland  but  I  have  been  unable

to  trace  the  publication  in  which  it  appeared.    An

appreciation  of  LEWIS  GRASSIC  GIBBON  (J.    LESLIE

MITCHELL)  AFTER  HIS  DEATH  by  EDWIN  MUIR  appears  in

the  same  issue  suggesting  a  date  of  1936.


D42

POWER, PRIDE AND PREJUDICE |

THE SCOTS MAGAZINE | DUNDEE

VOL 26   NO 5 PP 330 - 332                    FEBRUARY 1937

Published anonymously (by an Inverness Correspondent)

D43

INVERNESS AND ROUND ABOUT |

S.M.T. MAGAZINE | EDINBURGH |

VOL 18   NO 2   PP 14 - 17                    FEBRUARY 1937


D44

"GENTLEMEN - THE TOURIST" THE NEW HIGHLAND TOAST |

THE SCOTS MAGAZINE | DUNDEE

VOL 26   NO 6   PP 410 - 415                  MARCH 1937


D45

A VISITOR FROM DENMARK | THE SCOTS MAGAZINE | DUNDEE

VOL 27   NO 1   PP 96 - 101                   MAY 1937


D46

IN THE HILLS | S.M.T. MAGAZINE | EDINBURGH

VOL 18   NO 5   P 24                          MAY 1937

One of a number of articles by famous persons in
this edition under the general heading of "Choosing
an Ideal Holiday".


D47

THE FAMILY BOAT | THE SCOTS MAGAZINE | DUNDEE

VOL 27   NO 3   PP 169 - 174                  JUNE 1937


D48

WHAT SCOTLAND OFFERS THE HOLIDAYMAKER |

S.M.T. MAGAZINE | EDINBURGH

VOL 19   NO 1   PP 21 - 25                    JULY 1937

D49

ONE FISHER WENT SAILING |

THE SCOTS MAGAZINE | DUNDEE

VOL 27   NO 6   PP 414 - 418                    SEPTEMBER 1937


D50                        (D91)

A DAY WITH THE SEINE NET |

THE GLASGOW HERALD | GLASGOW

P 4                                        18TH SEPTEMBER 1937

P 4                                        25TH SEPTEMBER 1937


D51

THE FERRY OF THE DEAD |

THE SCOTS MAGAZINE | DUNDEE

VOL 28   NO 1   PP 13 - 20                       OCTOBER 1937


D52

SCOTLAND NORTH OF THE GRAMPIANS |

SCOTLAND | GLASGOW

VOL 2   NO 8   PP 6 - 11                          WINTER 1937

"Scotland" was the organ of the Scottish National
Development Council.


D53                        (A71)

THE TORRANAN ROCKS |

THE SCOTS MAGAZINE | DUNDEE

VOL 28   NO 4   PP 275 - 286                     JANUARY 1938

A travellers tale which was to form part of:-

OFF IN A BOAT | FABER & FABER | 5.5.1938 | PP 239 - 255

D54                          (A71)

SUMMER ADVENTURES IN WESTERN WATERS |

S.M.T. MAGAZINE | EDINBURGH

VOL 20   NO 1   PP 31 - 35                JANUARY 1938


D55

EIRE | THE SCOTS MAGAZINE | DUNDEE

VOL 28   NO 5   PP 340 - 344              FEBRUARY 1938


D56

SCOT WELCOME | SCOTTISH FIELD | GLASGOW

NO 423   PP 20 - 21                       MARCH 1938


D57

THE FIRST SALMON | THE SCOTS MAGAZINE | DUNDEE

VOL 29   NO 1   PP 17 - 20                APRIL 1938


D58

TOWN PLANNING IN THE SCOTTISH HIGHLANDS |

TOWN AND COUNTRY PLANNING | LONDON

VOL 6   NO 23   P 58                      APRIL-JUNE 1938


D59

THE WESTERN ISLES

A typescript with the above title is held at the
National Library of Scotland.

From internal evidence this relates to the "Off In A
Boat" period and can therefore be dated no later
than publication date 5.5.1938.

D60

PRESIDENT OF EIRE |

THE SCOTS MAGAZINE | DUNDEE

VOL 29   NO 3   PP 177 - 180                    JUNE 1938

Written under the pseudonym of Dane McNeil.


D61

THE FISHERMEN OF THE NORTH EAST |

SCOTLAND | GLASGOW

VOL 3   NO 3   PP 13 - 16                    AUTUMN 1938

"Scotland" was the organ of the Scottish National
Development Council.


D62                    (D64, D67)

NATIONALISM IN WRITING - TRADITION AND

MAGIC IN THE WORK OF LEWIS GRASSIC GIBBON |

THE SCOTS MAGAZINE | DUNDEE

VOL 30   NO 1   PP 28 - 35                    OCTOBER 1938


D63

THE NEW COMMUNITY OF IONA |

THE SCOTS MAGAZINE | DUNDEE

VOL 30   NO 3   PP 169 - 174                    DECEMBER 1938

Written under the pseudonym of Dane McNeil.


D64                    (D62, D67)

NATIONALISM IN WRITING (2) : THE THEATRE SOCIETY

OF SCOTLAND | THE SCOTS MAGAZINE | DUNDEE

VOL 30   NO 3   PP 194 - 198                    DECEMBER 1938

D65

WAYFARING MEMORIES OF 1938 |

S.M.T. MAGAZINE | EDINBURGH |

VOL 22   NO 1   PP 65 - 68                    JANUARY 1939


D66

AS DRUNK AS A BAVARIAN |

THE SCOTS MAGAZINE | DUNDEE

VOL 31   NO 1   PP 30 - 35                      APRIL 1939


D67                    (D62, D64)

NATIONALISM IN WRITING (3):IS SCOTTISH INDIVIDUALISM

TO BE DEPLORED | THE SCOTS MAGAZINE | DUNDEE

VOL 31   NO 4   PP 275 - 282                     JULY 1939


D68

EAST TO BUCHAN | THE SCOTS MAGAZINE | DUNDEE

VOL 31   NO 6   PP 419 - 424                SEPTEMBER 1939


D69

WHERE WE STAND | THE SCOTS MAGAZINE | DUNDEE

VOL 32   NO 1   PP 1 - 5                       OCTOBER 1939

Written anonymously as part of the regular column
"SCOTLAND MONTH BY MONTH".


D70

.... AND THEN REBUILD IT | THE SCOTS MAGAZINE | DUNDEE

VOL 32   NO 3   PP 173 - 178                  DECEMBER 1939


D71                    (A113)

DECEMBER FLOWERS | THE SCOTS MAGAZINE | DUNDEE

VOL 32   NO 4   PP 282 - 286                    JANUARY 1940

One of a monthly series entitled "MEMORIES OF THE MONTH" witten under the pseudonym of Dane McNeil. The articles from this series and the later series "A COUNTRYMAN'S YEAR" formed the basis of "HIGHLAND PACK".


D72                         (A98, A113)

THE TRAGIC GOAT | THE GLASGOW HERALD | GLASGOW

P 3                                   10TH FEBRUARY 1940

This nature article is in a similar vein to the "MEMORIES OF THE MONTHS" and "A COUNTRYMAN'S YEAR" Series and the Goat in question intrudes into "HIGHLAND PACK".

A reminiscence which appears in this article was used again in "THE SERPENT".


D73                         (A113)

JANUARY ON THE MOORS |

THE SCOTS MAGAZINE | DUNDEE

VOL 32   NO 5   PP  336 - 339              FEBRUARY 1940

One of a monthly series entitled "MEMORIES OF THE MONTHS" written under the pseudonym of Dane McNeil. The articles from this series and the later series "A COUNTRYMAN'S YEAR" formed the basis of "HIGHLAND PACK".


D74                    (A113, B15, D136)

ISLANDS AND SEAS |

CHAMBERS'S JOURNAL | EDINBURGH

8TH SERIES   VOL 9

PUBLISHED IN FOUR PARTS:

PART I     From Stornoway to Bernera

           NO 512   PP 103 - 107   FEBRUARY 1940

PART II    Farewell to Bernera

           NO 518   PP 204 - 207   MARCH 1940

PART III   To the Flannan Isles

           NO 523   PP 285 - 288   APRIL 1940

PART IV    The Light That Failed

           NO 527   PP 348 - 351   MAY 1940

Much of the content of this series was included in the collection of Essays "HIGHLAND PACK".


D75                    (A113)

### THE FACTORS TALE |

### THE GLASGOW HERALD | GLASGOW

P 3                                    9TH MARCH 1940

This article was used as part of "HIGHLAND PACK".


D76

### FROM A HIGHLAND NOTEBOOK |

### THE SCOTS MAGAZINE | DUNDEE

VOL 32   NO 6   PP 469 - 472              MARCH 1940

Written anonymously.


D77                    (A113)

### FEBRUARY AND THE BIRDS |

### THE SCOTS MAGAZINE | DUNDEE

VOL 32   NO 6   PP 434-438                MARCH 1940

One of a monthly series entitled "MEMORIES OF THE
MONTHS" written under the pseudonym of Dane McNeil.
The articles from this series and the later series
"A COUNTRYMAN'S YEAR" formed the basis of "HIGHLAND
PACK".


D78             FROM A HIGHLAND NOTEBOOK |
                THE SCOTS MAGAZINE | DUNDEE
VOL 33   NO 1   PP 60 - 64                    APRIL 1940
Written anonymously.


D79                     (A113)
                MARCH AND THE DEAD EARTH |
                THE SCOTS MAGAZINE | DUNDEE
VOL 33   NO 1   PP 28 - 31                    APRIL 1940
One of a monthly series entitled "MEMORIES OF THE
MONTHS" written under the pseudonym of Dane McNeil.
The articles from this series and the later series
"A COUNTRYMAN'S YEAR" formed the basis of "HIGHLAND
PACK".


D80
    THE HERRING INDUSTRY : DEBT AND DECLINE OF THE
                SCOTTISH FISHERIES |
            THE GLASGOW HERALD | GLASGOW
P 4                                         7TH MAY 1940


D81
            FROM A HIGHLAND NOTEBOOK |
            THE SCOTS MAGAZINE | DUNDEE

VOL 33   NO 2   PP 142 - 146          MAY 1940

Written anonymously.


D82                    (A113)

APRIL AND HER TRUMPETS |

THE SCOTS MAGAZINE | DUNDEE

VOL 33   NO 2   PP 93 - 96           MAY 1940

One of a monthly series entitled "MEMORIES OF THE
MONTHS" written under the pseudonym of Dane McNeil.
The article from this series and the later series "A
COUNTRYMAN'S YEAR" formed the basis of "HIGHLAND
PACK".


D83

ON LOOKING AT THINGS |

THE SCOTS MAGAZINE | DUNDEE

VOL 33   NO 3   PP 170 - 174         JUNE 1940


D84                    (A113)

THE MERRIE MONTH OF MAY |

THE SCOTS MAGAZINE | DUNDEE

VOL 33   NO 3   PP 190 - 194         JUNE 1940

One of a monthly series entitled "MEMORIES OF THE
MONTHS" written under the pseudonym of Dane McNeil.
The articles from this series and the later series
"A COUNTRYMAN'S YEAR" formed the basis of "HIGHLAND
PACK".


D85

SECRET SESSION |

THE SCOTS MAGAZINE | DUNDEE

VOL 33   NO 4   PP 241 - 243                    JULY 1940

Written anonymously as part of the regular column
"SCOTLAND MONTH BY MONTH".


D86                      (A113)

### PRELUDE TO JUNE |

THE SCOTS MAGAZINE | DUNDEE

VOL 33   NO 4   PP 259 - 263                    JULY 1940

One of a monthly series entitled "MEMORIES OF THE
MONTHS" written under the pseudonym of Dane McNeil.
The articles from this series and the later series
"A COUNTRYMAN'S YEAR" formed the basis of "HIGHLAND
PACK".


D87                      (A113)

### IN THE WILDS OF SUTHERLAND |

S.M.T. MAGAZINE | EDINBURGH

VOL 26   NO 1   PP 22 - 27                      JULY 1940

This article was used as part of "HIGHLAND PACK".


D88                      (A63)

### AUTHENTIC WHISKY |

THE GLASGOW HERALD | GLASGOW

P 3                                    3RD AUGUST 1940


D89                      (A113)

### SAILING INTO JULY |

THE SCOTS MAGAZINE | DUNDEE

VOL 33   NO 5   PP 352 - 356                  AUGUST 1940

One of a monthly series entitled "MEMORIES OF THE MONTHS" written under the pseudonym of Dane McNeil. The articles in this series and the later series "A COUNTRYMAN'S YEAR" formed the basis of "HIGHLAND PACK".

D90                     THE FRENCH SMACK |

            THE SCOTS MAGAZINE | DUNDEE

VOL 33   NO 5   PP 366 - 370                AUGUST 1940


D91                     (D50)

     A MAN'S LIFE - SEINE-NET FISHING IN WAR TIME |

            THE GLASGOW HERALD | GLASGOW

P 3                                 7TH SEPTEMBER 1940


D92

                    ON MAGIC |

            THE SCOTS MAGAZINE | DUNDEE

VOL 33   NO 6   PP 433 - 436            SEPTEMBER 1940


D93                     (A113)

            AND THE RAINS CAME |

            THE SCOTS MAGAZINE | DUNDEE

VOL 33   NO 6   PP 445 - 448            SEPTEMBER 1940

One of a monthly series entitled "MEMORIES OF THE MONTHS" written under the pseudonym of Dane McNeil. The articles in this series and the later series "A COUNTRYMAN'S YEAR" formed the basis of "HIGHLAND PACK".

D94

A CRICK IN THE BACK : BOOKSHELF SOLILOQUY |

THE GLASGOW HERALD | GLASGOW

P 3                                    5TH OCTOBER 1940


D95                    (A113)

CLOSE BOSOM FRIENDS OF THE MATURING SUN |

THE SCOTS MAGAZINE | DUNDEE

VOL 34   NO 1   PP 14 - 18               OCTOBER 1940

One of a monthly series entitled "MEMORIES OF THE MONTHS" written under the pseudonym of Dane McNeil. The articles in this series and the later series "A COUNTRYMAN'S YEAR" formed the basis of "HIGHLAND PACK".


D96

ON BELIEF | THE SCOTS MAGAZINE | DUNDEE

VOL 34   NO 1   PP 51 - 55               OCTOBER 1940


D97

PEACE TIME JOURNEY | S.M.T. MAGAZINE | EDINBURGH

VOL 26   NO 4   PP 23 - 27               OCTOBER 1940


D98                    (A113)

LAND AND SEA TWIN HALVES OF THE MYSTERY |

THE SCOTS MAGAZINE | DUNDEE

VOL 34   NO 2   PP 118 - 122             NOVEMBER 1940

One of a monthly series entitled "MEMORIES OF THE MONTHS" written under the pseudonym of Dane McNeil. The articles in this series and the later series "A

COUNTRYMAN'S YEAR" formed the basis of "HIGHLAND PACK".

D99

ON TRADITION | THE SCOTS MAGAZINE | DUNDEE

VOL 34   NO 2   PP 131 - 134                NOVEMBER 1940

D100                    (A113)

THE FALL | THE SCOTS MAGAZINE | DUNDEE

VOL 34   NO 3   PP 182 - 186               DECEMBER 1940

One of a monthly series entitled "MEMORIES OF THE MONTHS" written under the pseudonym of Dane McNeil. The articles in this series and the later series "A COUNTRYMAN'S YEAR" formed the basis of "HIGHLAND PACK".

D101

DRAINS FOR THE KRAAL | THE GLASGOW HERALD | GLASGOW

P 3                              4TH JANUARY 1941

D102                    (A113)

A BALANCE SHEET | THE SCOTS MAGAZINE | DUNDEE

VOL 34   NO 4   PP 258 - 262               JANUARY 1941

One of a monthly series entitled "MEMORIES OF THE MONTHS" written under the pseudonym of Dane McNeil. The articles in this series and the later series "A COUNTRYMAN'S YEAR" formed the basis of "HIGHLAND PACK".

D103                    (A113)

MAKING A ROCK GARDEN | THE SCOTS MAGAZINE | DUNDEE

VOL 34   NO 5   PP 359 - 363                FEBRUARY 1941

One of a monthly series entitled "MEMORIES OF THE
MONTHS" written under the pseudonym of Dane McNeil.
The articles in this series and the later series "A
COUNTRYMAN'S YEAR" formed the basis of "HIGHLAND
PACK".


D104

THE STRATH OF KILDONAN | S.M.T. MAGAZINE | EDINBURGH

VOL 27   NO 2   PP 25 - 31                FEBRUARY 1941


D105                         (A113)

TALKING OF THE WEATHER | THE SCOTS MAGAZINE | DUNDEE

VOL 34   NO 6   PP 424 - 428                MARCH 1941

One of a monthly series entitled "MEMORIES OF THE
MONTHS" written under the pseudonym of Dane McNeil.
The articles in this series and the later series "A
COUNTRYMAN'S YEAR" formed the basis of "HIGHLAND
PACK".


D106

ON BACKGROUNDS | THE SCOTS MAGAZINE | DUNDEE

VOL 34   NO 6   PP 437 - 440                MARCH 1941


D107                         (A113)

THE INNOCENT BRIGHTNESS OF A NEW-BORN DAY IS LOVELY
            YET | THE SCOTS MAGAZINE | DUNDEE

VOL 35   NO 1   PP 10 - 14                APRIL 1941

One of a monthly series entitled "MEMORIES OF THE

MONTHS" written under the pseudonym of Dane McNeil.
The articles in this series and the later series "A
COUNTRYMAN'S YEAR" formed the basis of "HIGHLAND
PACK".

D108                    (A113)

    THE MOLE-CATCHER | THE GLASGOW HERALD | GLASGOW
P 3                              10TH MAY 1941
This nature article later appeared in "HIGHLAND
PACK".

D109                    (A113)

    MIDSUMMER OF FOXES AND WILD CATS |

        THE SCOTS MAGAZINE | DUNDEE
VOL 35   NO 2   PP 118 - 122              MAY 1941
One of a monthly series entitled "MEMORIES OF THE
MONTHS" written under the pseudonym of Dane McNeil.
The articles in this series and the later series
"A COUNTRYMAN'S YEAR" formed the basis of "HIGHLAND
PACK".

D110                    (A113)

    AMONG THE LAMBS | THE SCOTS MAGAZINE | DUNDEE
VOL 35   NO 3   PP 180 - 184              JUNE 1941
One of the monthly series entitled "MEMORIES OF THE
MONTHS" written under the pseudonym of Dane McNeil.
The articles from this series and the later series
"A COUNTRYMAN'S YEAR" formed the basis of "HIGHLAND
PACK".

D111

THIS NORTHLAND | PRISONERS OF WAR NEWS | ABERDEEN

VOL 2   NO 1   PP 2 - 4                    JUNE - JULY 1941


D112                    (A113)

OFF ON HOLIDAY | THE SCOTS MAGAZINE | DUNDEE

VOL 35   NO 4   PP 281 - 285                    JULY 1941

One of a monthly series entitled "MEMORIES OF THE MONTHS" written under the pseudonym of Dane McNeil. The articles in this series and the later series "A COUNTRYMAN'S YEAR" formed the basis of "HIGHLAND PACK".


D113

ON DESTRUCTION | THE SCOTS MAGAZINE | DUNDEE

VOL 35   NO 4   PP 290 - 294                    JULY 1941


D114

OVER THE ORD OF CAITHNESS | S.M.T. MAGAZINE |

EDINBURGH |

VOL 28   NO 1   PP 26 - 30                    JULY 1941


D115          (D23, D38, D168, D209)

MY BIT OF BRITAIN | THE FIELD | LONDON

VOL 178   NO 4623   PP 136 - 137      2ND AUGUST 1941


D116                    (A113)

AS THE GENTLE RAIN FROM HEAVEN | THE SCOTS MAGAZINE |

DUNDEE

VOL 35   NO 5   PP 341 - 345                    AUGUST 1941

One of a monthly series entitled "MEMORIES OF THE MONTHS" written under the pseudonym of Dane McNeil. The articles from this series and the later series "A COUNTRYMAN'S YEAR" formed the basis of "HIGHLAND PACK".

D117

    ON REVIEWING | THE SCOTS MAGAZINE | DUNDEE

VOL 35  NO 5  PP 364 - 367          AUGUST 1941

D118                  (A113)

    TEACHING THE YOUNG | THE SCOTS MAGAZINE | DUNDEE

VOL 35  NO 6  PP 411 - 415        SEPTEMBER 1941

One of a monthly series entitled "MEMORIES OF THE MONTHS" Written under the pseudonym of Dane McNeil. The articles from this series and the later series "A COUNTRYMAN'S YEAR" formed the basis of "HIGHLAND PACK".

D119

    TO LOCH TORRIDON | S.M.T. MAGAZINE | EDINBURGH

VOL 28  NO 3  PP 19 - 23        SEPTEMBER 1941

D120                  (A113)

    THE ROSE AT THE GABLE END | THE SCOTS MAGAZINE |

                  DUNDEE

VOL 36  NO 1  PP 25 - 28        OCTOBER 1941

One of a monthly series entitled "MEMORIES OF THE MONTHS" Written under the pseudonym of Dane McNeil. The articles from this series and the later series

"A COUNTRYMAN'S YEAR" formed the basis of "HIGHLAND PACK".

D121                          (A113)

HARVESTING THE GOLDEN GRAIN | THE SCOTS MAGAZINE |
DUNDEE

VOL 36   NO 2   PP 107 - 111                NOVEMBER 1941

One of a monthly series entitled "MEMORIES OF THE MONTHS" Written under the pseudonym of Dane McNeil. The articles from this series and the later series "A COUNTRYMAN'S YEAR" formed the basis of "HIGHLAND PACK".

D122                          (A113)

DUCKS AND DEER | THE SCOTS MAGAZINE | DUNDEE

VOL 36   NO 3   PP 184 - 188                DECEMBER 1941

One of a monthly series entitled "MEMORIES OF THE MONTHS" Written under the pseudonym of Dane McNeil. The articles from this series and the later series "A COUNTRYMAN'S YEAR" formed the basis of "HIGHLAND PACK".

D123                          (A113)

RED BERRY OF THE ROSES | THE SCOTS MAGAZINE | DUNDEE

VOL 36   NO 4   PP 265 - 269                JANUARY 1942

One of a monthly series entitled "A COUNTRYMAN'S YEAR" Written under the pseudonym of Dane McNeil. The articles from this series and the earlier series "MEMORIES OF THE MONTHS" formed the basis of "HIGHLAND PACK".

D124 (A113)

THE KEEPER IN WAR TIME | THE SCOTS MAGAZINE | DUNDEE

VOL 36   NO 5   PP 359 - 362                FEBRUARY 1942

One of a monthly series entitled "A COUNTRYMAN'S YEAR" Written under the pseudonym of Dane McNeil. The articles from this series and the earlier series "MEMORIES OF THE MONTHS" formed the basis of "HIGHLAND PACK".


D125 (A113)

THE SHIELING AND THE BOTHY | THE SCOTS MAGAZINE |

DUNDEE

VOL 36   NO 6   PP 457 - 460                MARCH 1942

One of a monthly series entitled "A COUNTRYMAN'S YEAR" Written under the pseudonym of Dane McNeil. The articles from this series and the earlier series "MEMORIES OF THE MONTHS" formed the basis of "HIGHLAND PACK".


D126

ROUND THE HIGHLANDS | PRISONERS OF WAR NEWS | ABERDEEN

VOL 3   NO 2   PP 90 - 92                    MARCH 1942


D127

INCIDENTS BY THE WAY | S.M.T. MAGAZINE | EDINBURGH

VOL 29   NO 3   PP 18 - 21                   MARCH 1942


D128 (A113)

PICTURES IN THE FROSTY AIR | THE SCOTS MAGAZINE |

DUNDEE

VOL 37  NO 1  PP 31 - 34                    APRIL 1942

One of a monthly series entitled "A COUNTRYMAN'S
YEAR" Written under the pseudonym of Dane McNeil.
The articles from this series and the earlier series
"MEMORIES OF THE MONTHS" formed the basis of
"HIGHLAND PACK".


D129                      (A113)

   CATCHING UP ON TIME | THE SCOTS MAGAZINE | DUNDEE
VOL 37  NO 2  PP 113 - 118                    MAY 1942

One of a monthly series entitled "A COUNTRYMAN'S
YEAR" written under the pseudonym of Dane McNeil.
The articles from this series and the earlier series
"MEMORIES OF THE MONTHS" formed the basis of
"HIGHLAND PACK".


D130

   THE ESSENCE OF NATIONALISM | THE SCOTS MAGAZINE |
                      DUNDEE
VOL 37  NO 3  PP 169 - 172                    JUNE 1942


D131                      (A113)

   EARLY SUNLIGHT | THE SCOTS MAGAZINE | DUNDEE
VOL 37  NO 3  PP 200 - 203                    JUNE 1942

One of a monthly series entitled "A COUNTRYMAN'S
YEAR" written under the pseudonym of Dane McNeil.
The articles from this series and the earlier series
"MEMORIES OF THE MONTHS" formed the basis of
"HIGHLAND PACK".

D132 (A113)

ON THE EDGE OF THE MOOR | THE SCOTS MAGAZINE | DUNDEE

VOL 37   NO 4   PP 291 - 295                    JULY 1942

One of a monthly series entitled "A COUNTRYMAN'S YEAR" written under the pseudonym of Dane McNeil. The articles from this series and the earlier series "MEMORIES OF THE MONTHS" formed the basis of "HIGHLAND PACK".

D133

THIS ENGLISH BUSINESS | THE SCOTS MAGAZINE | DUNDEE

VOL 37   NO 4   PP 295 - 299                    JULY 1942

D134 (A113)

THE HILL BURN | THE SCOTS MAGAZINE | DUNDEE

VOL 37   NO 5   PP 362 - 366                    AUGUST 1942

One of a monthly series entitled "A COUNTRYMAN'S YEAR" written under the pseudonym of Dane McNeil. The articles from this series and the earlier series "MEMORIES OF THE MONTHS" formed the basis of "HIGHLAND PACK".

D135

A STOICISM THAT TAKES A LOT OF BREAKING | LONDON
CALLING | LONDON

NO 159   PP 6 - 7                    24TH SEPTEMBER 1942

D136 (A113, D74)

ISLANDS AND SEAS | THE SCOTS MAGAZINE | DUNDEE

VOL 37   NO 6   PP 445 - 449                    SEPTEMBER 1942

One of a monthly series entitled "A COUNTRYMAN'S

YEAR" written under the pseudonym of Dane McNeil.
The articles from this series and the earlier series
"MEMORIES OF THE MONTHS" formed the basis of
"HIGHLAND PACK".

D137

BLACK CATTLE IN LOCHABER | THE SCOTS MAGAZINE | DUNDEE
VOL 37   NO 6   PP 450 - 454                SEPTEMBER 1942

D138

    FISHING LOCHS OF DAY AND NIGHT | S.M.T. MAGAZINE |
                      EDINBURGH
VOL 30   NO 3   PP 13 - 15                  SEPTEMBER 1942

D139                         (A113)
    A FIELD OF OATS | THE SCOTS MAGAZINE | DUNDEE
VOL 38   NO 1   PP 42 - 46                   OCTOBER 1942
One of a monthly series entitled "A COUNTRYMAN'S
YEAR" written under the pseudonym of Dane McNeil.
The articles from this series and the earlier series
"MEMORIES OF THE MONTHS" formed the basis of
"HIGHLAND PACK".

D140                         (A113, B22)
DANCING IN THE HIGHLANDS | THE SCOTS MAGAZINE | DUNDEE
VOL 38   NO 1   PP 46 - 50                   OCTOBER 1942

D141                         (A113)
    A RABBIT IN A SNARE | THE SCOTS MAGAZINE | DUNDEE
VOL 38   NO 2   PP 123 - 126                NOVEMBER 1942

One of a monthly series entitled "A COUNTRYMAN'S YEAR" written under the pseudonym of Dane McNeil. The articles from this series and the earlier series "MEMORIES OF THE MONTHS" formed the basis of "HIGHLAND PACK".

D142                    (A113)

WORKING ON SUNDAYS | THE SCOTS MAGAZINE | DUNDEE
VOL 38   NO 3   PP 209 - 212          DECEMBER 1942
One of a monthly series entitled "A COUNTRYMAN'S YEAR" written under the pseudonym of Dane McNeil. The articles from this series and the earlier series "MEMORIES OF THE MONTHS" formed the basis of "HIGHLAND PACK".

D143

MORE FISHING LOCHS - AND A FEAST! | S.M.T. MAGAZINE |
                    EDINBURGH
VOL 31   NO 2   PP 13 - 15            FEBRUARY 1943

D144                    (A113)

DEATH OF THE LAMB | THE SCOTS MAGAZINE | DUNDEE
VOL 39   NO 1   PP 33 - 36            APRIL 1943

D145

WE MUST HAVE A LOT MORE FUN IN LIVING | DAILY RECORD |
                    GLASGOW
NO 30072   P 2                       10TH JUNE 1943

D146

ROUND THE BLACK ISLE | S.M.T. MAGAZINE | EDINBURGH

VOL 32   NO 1   PP 20 - 22                    JULY 1943


D147

SCOTLAND MOVES | THE SCOTS MAGAZINE | DUNDEE

VOL 39   NO 6   PP 447 - 450              SEPTEMBER 1943


D148

NOT SO STERN AND WILD | DAILY RECORD | GLASGOW

NO 30424   P 2                        26TH JULY 1944


D149

- AND AFTER THE WAR | DAILY RECORD | GLASGOW

NO 30438   P 2                        11TH AUGUST 1944


D150

NEW CHARTER BEHIND "IFS" | DAILY RECORD | GLASGOW

NO 30447   P 2                        22ND AUGUST 1944


D151

THE HEALTH SERVICE WE WANT | DAILY RECORD | GLASGOW

NO 30455   P 2                        31ST AUGUST 1944


D152

A LEAGUE OF FISHERMEN | DAILY RECORD | GLASGOW

NO 30461   P 2                        7TH SEPTEMBER 1944


D153

EXCITING HORIZONS | DAILY RECORD | GLASGOW

NO 30468   P 2                        15TH SEPTEMBER 1944

D154

PLANNERS AND PEOPLE | DAILY RECORD | GLASGOW

NO 30485   P 2                    5TH OCTOBER 1944


D155

HIMMLER PUTS IT A NEW WAY | DAILY RECORD | GLASGOW

NO 30492   P 2                    13TH OCTOBER 1944


D156

THE MORAL OF THE MIDGE | DAILY RECORD | GLASGOW

NO 30496   P 2                    18TH OCTOBER 1944


D157

SCOTS ARE CRITICAL TOO SOON | DAILY RECORD | GLASGOW

NO 30510   P 2                    3RD NOVEMBER 1944


D158

QUESTIONS FOR SCOTS | DAILY RECORD | GLASGOW

NO 30528   P 2                    24TH NOVEMBER 1944


D159

TWEEDS AS A TEST FOR GOODWILL | DAILY RECORD | GLASGOW

NO 30538   P 2                    6TH DECEMBER 1944


D160

AWAKENING OF A NATION | DAILY RECORD | GLASGOW

NO 30556   P 2                    27TH DECEMBER 1944


D161

SCOTLAND ISN'T A "REGION" | DAILY RECORD | GLASGOW
NO 30571   P 2                        15TH JANUARY 1945


D162

   LONDON'S ETERNAL PRIORITY | DAILY RECORD | GLASGOW
NO 30593   P 2                        9TH FEBRUARY 1945


D163

   TAKE THE HILL PATH | S.M.T. MAGAZINE | EDINBURGH
VOL 35   NO 2   PP 13 - 15            FEBRUARY 1945


D164

   THE MONTH IN SCOTLAND | SCOTTISH FIELD | GLASGOW
VOL 93   NO 513   P 9                 SEPTEMBER 1945


D165

   BELIEF IN OURSELVES | THE SCOTS MAGAZINE | DUNDEE
VOL 43   NO 6   PP 424 - 427          SEPTEMBER 1945


D166

   THE NOVEL AT HOME | THE SCOTS MAGAZINE | DUNDEE
VOL 45   NO 1   PP 1 - 5                 APRIL 1946
This article later appeared in:-
THE WRITER | BOSTON | JUNE 1946 | VOL 59 | NO 6 |
PP 179 - 181
The article was originally written for the latter
Magazine.


D167                      (A84)

   FILMING THE SILVER DARLINGS | S.M.T. MAGAZINE |

EDINBURGH

VOL 38   NO 3   PP 21 - 23                SEPTEMBER 1946


D168            (D23, D38, D115, D209)

THE CAITHNESS COAST | SCOTLANDS MAGAZINE | EDINBURGH

VOL 39   NO 1   PP 24 - 27                JANUARY 1947


D169

NOTE ON THE BASKING SHARK

NO   DATE

The above unpublished article is held in typescript
form   at   the   National   Library   of   Scotland.
From   the   address   it   is   evidently   pre   1948.


D170

EDINBURGH | HOLIDAY | PHILADELPHIA

VOL 4   NO 2   PP 90 - 104                AUGUST 1948

Typescript held at the National Library of Scotland.


D171

CALVINISM AND CRITICS | JABBERWOCK | EDINBURGH

VOL 2   NO 4   PP 2 - 4                FEBRUARY 1949

Jabberwock was the name of the Edinburgh University
Review.


D172

IT'S BETTER THAN EVER | DAILY RECORD | GLASGOW

NO 16626   P 2                19TH FEBRUARY 1949


D173

HISTORY HEARD TO LAUGH | THE GLASGOW HERALD | GLASGOW

P 3                                         24TH DECEMBER 1949


D174

I'VE GOT MY BENT 3D BIT YET | SCOTTISH DAILY EXPRESS |

                            GLASGOW

P 4                                         27TH DECEMBER 1949


D175

    GIANTS AND DISTANT BELLS | THE GLASGOW HERALD |

                        GLASGOW

P 3                                         18TH FEBRUARY 1950

One page of typescript held at the National Library

of Scotland.


D176

    TOWARDS CAPE WRATH | SCOTLANDS MAGAZINE | EDINBURGH

VOL 45   NO 2   PP 24 - 29                   FEBRUARY 1950

Typescript held at National Library of Scotland.


D177

        WILD SWANS | THE SCOTS REVIEW | GLASGOW

VOL 11   NO 1   P 3                          APRIL 1950


D178                        (A121, E14)

    THE PURSUIT OF LIGHT | SCOTLANDS MAGAZINE | EDINBURGH

VOL 45   NO 4   PP 38 - 41                   APRIL 1950

Reflects the opening scene of "THE WELL AT THE

WORLD'S END"

D179

ENGLISH CRITICS AND SCOTS NOVELISTS | JABBERWOCK |

EDINBURGH

VOL 3   NO 2   PP 7 - 8                         MAY 1950

This is a reply to an article "SCOTS BARDS AND ENGLISH REVIEWERS" by "Charpie" in Jabberwock Vol 3 No 1 PP 17 - 18. Which was in turn a reply to the article "CALVINISM AND CRITICS" by NEIL GUNN in the Feb. 1949 Jabberwock.

D180

ACROSS KYLESCU | SCOTLANDS MAGAZINE | EDINBURGH

VOL 45   NO 6   PP 24 - 28                       JUNE 1950

Typescript held at National Library of Scotland.

D181

LIVING IN THE FREE SUNLIGHT | THE GLASGOW HERALD |

GLASGOW

P 3                                    22ND JULY 1950

D182

OFF TO ULLAPOOL | SCOTLANDS MAGAZINE | EDINBURGH

VOL 46   NO 4   PP 24 - 28                     OCTOBER 1950

D183

SCOTLAND | HOLIDAY | PHILADELPHIA

VOL 8   NO 6   PP 34 - 47, 101, 102, 104, 107

DECEMBER   1950

This article later appeared in:-

TEN YEARS OF HOLIDAY | SIMON AND SCHUSTER | NEW YORK |

1956 | PP 114 - 132

ROUND THE WORLD WITH FAMOUS AUTHORS | DOUBLEDAY,    IN
ASSOCIATION WITH PAN AMERICAN WORLD AIRWAYS | NEW
YORK | 1958 | P 42 (A 16 LINE EXTRACT ONLY APPEARED IN
THIS ANTHOLOGY)
THE WORLD OF MANKIND | GOLDEN PRESS | NEW YORK | 1962 |
PP 28 - 33


D184

   PICTS HOUSES | SCOTLANDS MAGAZINE | EDINBURGH
VOL 47   NO 2   PP 37 - 39                FEBRUARY 1951


D185

REACHES OF THE CONON | SCOTLANDS MAGAZINE | EDINBURGH
VOL 47   NO 4   PP 41 - 43                 APRIL 1951


D186

   INVERNESS AND THE HIGHLANDS | SCOTLANDS MAGAZINE |
                     EDINBURGH
VOL 47   NO 5   PP 29 - 33                 MAY 1951


D187                    (A113)
      A DELICACY OF EXCHANGE | THE GLASGOW HERALD |
                     GLASGOW
   P 3                         17TH NOVEMBER 1951
An   essay   in   the   same   mould   as   those   used   in
"HIGHLAND PACK".


D188

   AWAY TO THE ISLES | SCOTLANDS MAGAZINE | EDINBURGH

156

D189                    (A113)

DANCING IN THE WILDS | THE GLASGOW HERALD | GLASGOW

P 3                                    31ST MAY 1952

Manuscript held at the National Library of Scotland.
An  essay  in  the  same  mould  as  those  used  in
"HIGHLAND PACK".


D190


SALUTE  TO  A  MIRACLE | THE GLASGOW HERALD | GLASGOW

P 3                                   16TH AUGUST 1952

An  essay  on  the  effects  of  the  Hydro-electric
programme on the salmon runs.


D191

    THE HIGHLANDS TODAY | THE GEOGRAPHICAL MAGAZINE |
                        LONDON

VOL 25   NO 5   PP 232 - 241          SEPTEMBER 1952

Typescript held at National Library of Scotland.


D192

    THE GREAT GLEN AFFRIC SCHEME | THE SPHERE | LONDON

VOL 211   NO 2748   PP 58 - 63        11TH OCTOBER 1952

Typescript held at National Library of Scotland.


D193

               ABOVE THE HIGHLAND LINE

A  printed  copy  exists  in  the  National  Library  of

Scotland comprising pages 26-29 of a publication so far unidentified. From internal evidence this was commissioned by the Scottish Tourist Board and may have formed part of a Publicity Brochure. An approach to the Tourist Board has failed to trace but, from references to a Hydro-electric scheme believed to be that of Glen Affric, this must have been written prior to 1952

D194


THE GREAT GLEN OF SCOTLAND | THE SPHERE | LONDON
VOL 213   NO 2785   PP 602 - 605          27TH JUNE 1953
Typescript held at National Library of Scotland.


D195

THE SHOELACE AND THE SALMON | SCOTLANDS MAGAZINE |
EDINBURGH
VOL 49   NO 8   PP 56 - 59                AUGUST 1953
Article on Salmon Poaching.
Typescript held at the National Library of Scotland under the title "Poaching".


D196

BEAUTIFUL BALMORAL | HOLIDAY | PHILADELPHIA
VOL 16   NO 2   PP 74 - 78                AUGUST 1954


D197

THE CLANS OF SCOTLAND | HOLIDAY | PHILADELPHIA
VOL 16   NO 3   PP 38 - 45, 63 - 64, 66, 69

Typescript held at National Library of Scotland.

D198                    (A59, B24, E25)

    THE TRAGEDY OF THE HIGHLAND CLEARANCES |

    RADIO TIMES (SCOTTISH EDITION) | LONDON

VOL 125   NO 1622   P 5                    10TH DECEMBER 1954

D199

    CURLING | UNPUBLISHED ARTICLE

                                            1954

Produced  for  Time  Life  Magazine  in  the  U.S.A  but
never published.


Typescript held at the National Library of Scotland.


D200

BOOKS  :  NEIL  M.  GUNN  TALKS  ABOUT  SOME  OLD  SCOTS
BOOKS
Article forms P.12 of an unidentified Newspaper.
The  books  in  question  were  "CARMINA  GADELICA"  and
"THE   GRAMPIANS   DESOLATE"   (1804)   by   ALEXANDER
CAMPBELL.   GUNN  talks  of  this  being  150  years  ago
which suggests a probable date of 1954.


D201

    IN THE HIGHLANDS | SPECTATOR | LONDON

VOL 194   NO 6626   PP XVI - XVIII - INSERT AFTER PAGE
798                                   24TH JUNE 1955
(Part of "PROSPECT OF SCOTLAND" series of inserts).

D202

WHEN I GO FISHING | TROUT AND SALMON | PETERBOROUGH

VOL 1    NO 2    PAGE 11                          AUGUST 1955

Typescript held at National Library of Scotland.


D203

THE SCOTS ARE CLANSMEN STILL | EVERYBODY'S WEEKLY |

LONDON

PP 19 - 21, 37                          10TH SEPTEMBER 1955


D204

OFF IN THE CAR | FROM "THE SCOTTISH COMPANION"

- ED. RHODA SPENCE | RICHARD PATERSON LTD |

EDINBURGH | 1955

PP 1 - 6

Typescript held at National Library of Scotland.


D205

PRESCRIPTIONS | MEDICAL WORLD | LONDON

VOL 84    NO 2    PP 160 - 167                FEBRUARY 1956

Typescript held at the National Library of Scotland.


D206

LIVING IN SCOTLAND TODAY | SCOTTISH FIELD |

GLASGOW

VOL 104    NO 638    PP 51 - 53              FEBRUARY 1956


D207                        (A127)

THE EVIL EYE | SALTIRE REVIEW | EDINBURGH

An extract in advance from the ATOM OF DELIGHT.


D208                    (A127)

EXTRACTS FROM "THE ATOM OF DELIGHT" | THE GLASGOW

HERALD | GLASGOW

1) Off and Away          P 3      22ND SEPTEMBER 1956

2) Trees in Church       P 3      29TH SEPTEMBER 1956

3) The Family Cow        P 3      6TH OCTOBER 1956

4) The Boy in London     P 3      13TH OCTOBER 1956


D209          (D23, D38, D115, D168)

CAITHNESS | COUNTRY FAIR | LONDON

VOL 11   NO 6   PP I - VIII   (99 - 106)   DECEMBER 1956

This was Country Fair Supplement No 66 - A series on

Counties round Britain.

Typescript held at National Library of Scotland.


D210                    (A63)

WHISKY

From  correspondence  it  seems  that  an  article  so

entitled appeared both in "Edinburgh Year Book 1956"

and "Scottish Industrial Guide".

Both  were  published  by  SCOTT HAMILTON (PUBLISHERS)

LTD - 25 York Place Edinburgh | but    I    have    been

unable to trace copies.

A typescript with this title is held at the National

Library of Scotland which may relate.


D211

IONA | UNPUBLISHED ARTICLE

1956

Produced for the American "HOUSE AND GARDEN" Magazine but seemingly never published.

Typescript held at the National Library of Scotland.


D212        (A74, A80, B14, B29, E44)

DEER STALKING IN THE HIGHLANDS | HOLIDAY |

PHILADELPHIA

VOL 21   NO 1   PP 60 - 61, 126, 129      JANUARY 1957

Typescript held at the National Library of Scotland.


D213        (D11, D217, E42)

FOR CHRISTOPHER'S CAP | UNPUBLISHED

JULY  1957

This piece was written in honour of Christopher Grieve's Honorary Doctorate at Edinburgh University. It seems probable that this was in fact the text of the B.B.C. Programme of 3rd July 1957 entitled "THE INDIVISIBLE MAN - MEN OF MARK" but, as no script remains for that, this cannot be confirmed.

Typescript held at the National Library of Scotland.


D214            (A127)

THE HERONS LEGS | SALTIRE REVIEW | EDINBURGH

VOL 5   NO 15   PP 19 - 22            SUMMER 1958

One of six philosophical/autobiographical articles published by this magazine which continue the themes explored in "The Atom of Delight". These are further continued in "Point" Magazine in two articles in 1968 - 1969.


D215                    (A127)

    THE FLASH | SALTIRE REVIEW | EDINBURGH

VOL 5   NO 16   PP 18 - 23                    AUTUMN 1958

One of six philosophical/autobiographical articles
published by this magazine which continue the themes
explored in "The Atom of Delight". These are
further continued in "Point" Magazine in two
articles in 1968 - 1969.


D216                    (A127)

    EIGHT TIMES UP | SALTIRE REVIEW | EDINBURGH

VOL 5   NO 17   PP 19 - 23                    WINTER 1958

One of six philosophical/autobiographical articles
published by this magazine which continue the themes
explored in "The Atom of Delight". These are
further continued in "Point" Magazine in two
articles in 1968 - 1969.


D217                 (D11, D213, E42)

    ON HUGH MACDIARMID | JABBERWOCK | EDINBURGH

VOL 5   NO 1   P 11                               1958


D218                    (A63)

    MALT WHISKIES | SCOTLANDS MAGAZINE | EDINBURGH

VOL 55   NO 2   P 47                    FEBRUARY 1959

Typescript held at National Library of Scotland.


D219                    (A127)

REMEMBER YOURSELF | SALTIRE REVIEW | EDINBURGH

VOL 6   NO 18   PP 22 - 28                        SPRING 1959

One of six philosophical/autobiographical articles published by this magazine which continue the themes explored in "The Atom of Delight".   These are further continued in "Point" Magazine in two articles in 1968 - 1969.


D220                        (A71, E54)

    THE LIGHT OF IONA | THE LISTENER | LONDON

VOL 61   PP 1061 - 1062                        18TH JUNE 1959

A transcript of the talk of the same title which was narrated by GUNN on the Third Programme of the BBC 5.6.1959.


D221                        (A127)

    LANDSCAPE INSIDE | SALTIRE REVIEW | EDINBURGH

VOL 6   NO 19   PP 43 - 46                        AUTUMN 1959

(Thoughts from an unscripted BBC talk with George Bruce)

One of six philosophical/autobiographical articles published by this magazine which continue the themes explored in "The Atom of Delight".   These are further continued in "Point" Magazine in two articles in 1968 - 1969.


D222

    HIGH ON THE HAGGIS | HOLIDAY | PHILADELPHIA

VOL 26   NO 5   PP94-97, 130-131                        NOVEMBER 1959

Typescript held at National Library of Scotland

under title "Scottish Food".

D223

### HIGH SUMMER BY A MOUNTAIN LOCHAN |

### SCOTLANDS MAGAZINE | EDINBURGH

VOL 56   NO 6   PP 10-11                    JUNE 1960

This piece accompanies a photograph of Loch A'an and was condensed from a longer article entitled "Loch A'an" the typescript of which is held at the National Library of Scotland.

D224

THE DORNOCH FIRTH | SCOTLANDS MAGAZINE | EDINBURGH

VOL 56   NO 10   PP 22-27                    OCTOBER 1960

Typescript held at National Library of Scotland.

D225                    (A63)

THE LONG JOHN STORY | LONG JOHN DISTILLERIES | GLASGOW

7TH OCTOBER 1960

This booklet was published anonymously but a copy of a typescript is held at the National Library of Scotland.   It was originally produced as an official programme for the opening of Seager, Evans Ltd (now Long John International Ltd's) new malt distillery at Tormore.   The text continued to be incorporated in the Company's publicity material for a number of years but has now been superceded.

When Tormore Distillery was officially opened a 'Time Capsule' in the form of a pot still was buried in the forecourt of the Distillery.   This contained a recording of chimes used in their clock, a Tregnum of Long John Whisky, a treatise on how scotch is made, a history of the whisky industry, names of plant employees, an American Dollar, the names of all the Scottish Clans and samples of grain, water, peat and cask staves. It is believed that a copy of this booklet is included.

D226

## PIGS AND WHISTLES

Typescript held at the National Library of Scotland - no date. It is a light hearted article on the difficulties of receiving Third Programme Broadcasts in the Highlands.

From the address the article must be 1950-1960.

D227

## UNIVERSITY OF INVERNESS

A typescript with the above title is held at the National Library of Scotland.

The typescript is noted in Gunn's hand 'First Memorandum prepared (1960) for Provost Wotherspoon who will present copy to reps. of Univ. Grants Comm.'

D228

"TOWNSCAPES" - INVERNESS - CROSSROADS OF THE NORTHERN KINGDOM | THE SCOTSMAN - WEEKEND MAGAZINE | EDINBURGH NO 36763  PAGE 1 (17 OF OVERALL NEWSPAPER)

25TH MARCH 1961

Typescript held at National Library of Scotland.

D229

CONVERSATION WITH A NOVELIST | SCOTTISH FIELD |
GLASGOW

VOL 108   NO 701   PP 38-39 + 111            MAY 1961

A conversation between Maurice Lindsay and Neil M.
Gunn prepared by Maurice Lindsay.

Typescript held at the National Library of Scotland.


D230

BY PASTURES GREEN | OSSIAN | GLASGOW

NO 4   PP 6-8                              AUTUMN 1961

Typescript held at the National Library of Scotland.


D231

THE PEACEFUL BLACK ISLE | SCOTLANDS MAGAZINE |
EDINBURGH

VOL 57   NO 10   PP 20-25              OCTOBER 1961

Typescript held at the National Library of Scotland.


D232                    (A127)

HIGHLAND SPACE | SALTIRE REVIEW | EDINBURGH

VOL 6   NO 23   PP 45-48                  WINTER 1961

One of six philosphical/autobiographical articles
published by this magazine which continue the themes
explored in "The Atom of Delight". These are
further continued in "Point" Magazine in two
articles in 1968-1969.

Typescript held at the National Library of Scotland.

D233

### THE HIGHLANDS OF SCOTLAND | MERIAN

4TH JUNE 1962

This was an article in German in a German Magazine. A typescript of an English version is held on deposit by The National Library of Scotland.

D234                      (A84)

### THE SILVER FISH | RADIO TIMES (SCOTTISH EDITION) |
### LONDON

VOL 156   NO 2025   P18                      30TH AUGUST 1962

D235

### SCOTTISH RENAISSANCE | SCOTTISH FIELD | GLASGOW

VOL 109   NO 716   P34                      AUGUST 1962

A typescript of this article is held at the National Library of Scotland under the title "Hugh MacDiarmid".

D236                      (A63)

### AN AFFAIR OF WHISKY | NEW SALTIRE | EDINBURGH

NO 6   PP6-11                      DECEMBER 1962

D237

### THE LINGERING PROBLEM OF THE HIGHLANDS |
### THE GLASGOW HERALD | GLASGOW

P6                      10TH DECEMBER 1966

D238

A FOOTNOTE ON CO-OPERATION | ANARCHY 86 | LONDON

VOL 8   NO 4   PP 116-117                    APRIL 1968


D239              (E53 E59 E72)

THE WONDER STORY OF THE MORAY FIRTH | ANARCHY 86 |

LONDON

VOL 8   NO 4   PP 122-125                    APRIL 1968

This first appeared as a Radio Programme on 28th
April 1959.


D240              (A127)

LIGHT | POINT | LEICESTER

NO 3   PP 4-12                               SUMMER 1968

One of two philosophical/autobiographical articles
published by this magazine which continue the themes
explored in "The Atom of Delight" and six articles
in "Saltire Review".


D241              (A127)

THE MIRACULOUS | POINT | LEICESTER

NO 4   PP 19-27                              WINTER 1968-69

One of two philosophical/autobiographical articles
published by this magazine which continue the themes
explored in "The Atom of Delight" and six articles
in "Saltire Review".

Typescript held at National Library of Scotland.


D242              (A121 E94 E96)

STRANGE HAPPENINGS IN THE HIGHLANDS | RADIO TIMES

(SCOTTISH EDITION) | LONDON

VOL 186   NO 2416   P12          26TH FEBRUARY 1970

An article prepared by Deirdre MacDonald comprising a conversation between herself and Neil M. Gunn to publicise the adaptation of the novel "The Well at the Worlds End" for Broadcasting.


D243

### BALMORAL: HUNTING IN THE HIGHLANDS
### BALMORAL

Two typescripts, one incomplete, bearing the above titles are held at the National Library of Scotland. Whilst exploring a similar theme these do not appear to relate directly to the "Holiday" article entitled "Beautiful Balmoral" which appeared in August 1954.


D244

### THE COUNTY BEHIND THE CAMERONS | UNPUBLISHED ARTICLE

Typescript held at the National Library of Scotland.


D245

### FISHING | UNPUBLISHED

There is a suggestion that this paper was written with a view to interesting commercial T.V. in the state of the fishing industry. There is no indication of date other than the fact that there was an Icelandic dispute going on at the time. Typescript held at the National Library of Scotland.


170

D246

THE GATHERING OF THE CAMERONS | UNPUBLISHED ARTICLE

Typescript held at the National Library of Scotland. Written in advance of a Clan gathering and giving a synopsis of their involvement under Lochiel in the '45. From the phraseology used this appears to have been aimed at the American Market but does not appear to have been published.

D247                    (A63)

HIGHLAND POT STILL MALT WHISKY | UNPUBLISHED ARTICLE

Typescript held at the National Library of Scotland.

D248

THE HIGHLANDS |

Appears on PP32-34 of an unidentified periodical. From the content the article was clearly written after completion of the Glen Affric Hydro-Electric Scheme and is therefore post 1952.

D249

HIGHLANDS AND ISLANDS

An undated typescript with the above title is held at the National Library of Scotland.

D250                    (D3)

HUNTING WITH HAWKS | UNPUBLISHED ARTICLE

Typescript held at the National Library of Scotland.

D251

LITERARY RETROSPECT

No Date

A Typescript of the above article, believed to be unpublished, is held at the National Library of Scotland.

It takes the form of potted book reviews and recollections on:-

'THE DARK CHILD'        -    CAMARA LAYE
'THE LITTLE ARK'        -    JAN DE HARTOG
'THE SUPREME DOCTRINE'  -    HUBERT BENOIT


D252

LITERATURE AND THE ARTS

No Date

A typescript of the above paper, believed to be unpublished, is held at the National Library of Scotland.

It is a paper outlining suggestions for arts programmes clearly intended for the B.B.C.


D253

THE MYTH OF THE CANNY SCOT | UNPUBLISHED ARTICLE

Typescript held at the National Library of Scotland. From the phraseology used this appears to have been aimed at the American market but does not appear to have been published.


D254

THE MYTH OF THE GLOOMY SCOT | UNPUBLISHED ARTICLE

Typescript held at the National Library of Scotland.

From the phraseology used this appears to have been aimed at the American market but does not appear to have been published.

D255

### THE OBVIOUS

Undated manuscript held at the National Library of Scotland.

Refers to Ouspensky's Book "In Search of the Miraculous" and must therefore be post 1950.

D256

### THE ONE WHO WILL COME | UNPUBLISHED ARTICLE

Manuscript and typescript held at the National Library of Scotland.

D257

### RED DEER IN SCOTLAND

A typescript with the above title is held at the National Library of Scotland. It is a detailed assessment, arguing the case that powers granted under the 'Agriculture (Scotland) Act 1948' to the various agriculture executive committees is too absolute and advocating a return to the laws operating pre 1939.

D258                        (A63)

### WHISKY AND SCOTLAND

A typescript with the above title is held at the National Library of Scotland. Evidently post war.

D259

### WHY ARE WRITERS NATIONALISTS | SCOTS INDEPENDENT | STIRLING

p7

I have been unable to trace an exact date for this article but it is evidently post 1940.


D260

### WILLIAM SOUTAR

A typescript with the above title is held at the National Library of Scotland.


D261

### WOMAN'S VIEWPOINT

A typescript with the above title is held at the National Library of Scotland.

This seems to have been a paper produced for the B.B.C. concerning a possible series of Radio Programes.

E

BROADCAST MATERIAL

El

SCOTLAND TODAY IX - "LITERATURE"

12TH MARCH 1929

TYPE OF WORK      -      TALK

PRODUCER         -      NOT KNOWN

PROGRAMME        -      SCOTTISH REGIONAL PROGRAMME

TIME             -      15 MINUTES

No known typescript or recording held.


E2                    (A40 B1)

THE HAWKS FEATHER

24TH SEPTEMBER 1929

For details see entry under plays for August 1929.


E3                    (A58 B7 B12)

OLD MUSIC

19TH JUNE 1936

For details see entry under plays for July 1935.


E4        (A24 A33 A34 A51 A107 B5 E11 E36 E58)

BACK HOME

16TH AUGUST 1937

For details see entry under plays for 1932.


E5                    (B15)

THE LAND WE DEFEND: THE WESTERN HIGHLANDS AND ISLANDS

30TH AUGUST 1940

For details see entry under plays for 30.8.1940.


E6                    (B16 B17)

LEWIS TODAY

10TH   DECEMBER   1941

For details see entry under plays for 10.12.1941.


E7                      (B18)

HIGHLAND PROSPECT

10TH   OCTOBER   1942

For details see entry under plays for 10.10.1942.


E8                  (A31 A76 B20)

THE BLACK WOOLLEN GLOVES

8TH   FEBRUARY   1944

For details see entry under plays for 8.2.1944.


E9          (A96 A112 A130 B21 E10 E33 E71)

SUN AND MOON

1ST   JUNE   1944

For details see entry under plays for 1.6.1944.


E10         (A96 A112 A130 B21 E9 E33 E71)

SUN AND MOON

6TH   FEBRUARY   1947

Repeat of Broadcast of 1.6.1944.


E11     (A24 A33 A34 A51 A107 B5 E4 E36 E58)

TILLEADH DHACHAIDH (GAELIC VERSION OF 'BACK HOME')

13TH   MARCH   1947

For details see entry under plays for 1932.


E12                     (A107)

THE TOAST IS SCOTLAND

30TH  NOVEMBER  1948

TYPE OF WORK      -    EXCERPT FROM 'THE DRINKING WELL'

PRODUCER          -    ROBIN RICHARDSON

PROGRAMME         -    SCOTTISH HOME SERVICE

TIME              -    EXTRACT - 2 MINUTES

Typescript held at B.B.C. Glasgow.


E13                      (A110)

"BOOK REVIEW" - THE SILVER BOUGH

10TH  DECEMBER  1948

TYPE OF WORK      -    REVIEW OF GUNN'S NEW BOOK BY

                      MAURICE LINDSAY.

PRODUCER          -    NOT KNOWN

PROGRAMME         -    SCOTTISH HOME SERVICE

TIME              -    15 MINUTES (TOTAL PROGRAMME)

No known typescript or recording held.


E14                      (A121 D178)

"SCOTTISH DIGEST" - THE PURSUIT OF LIGHT

11TH  APRIL  1950

TYPE OF WORK      -    DIGEST OF PERIODICALS (AN

                      ARTICLE OF THIS NAME APPEARED

                      IN SCOTLANDS MAGAZINE APRIL

                      1950)

PRODUCER          -    A.P.  LEE

PROGRAMME         -    SCOTTISH HOME SERVICE

TIME              -    30 MINUTES

No known typescript or recording held.

E15

INTERLUDE

24TH JUNE 1950

TYPE OF WORK    —    EXTRACT FROM STORM AND

PRECIPICE AND OTHER PIECES

PRODUCER    —    NOT KNOWN

PROGRAMME    —    THIRD

TIME    —    10 MINUTES

No known typescript or recording held.


E16    (A69 A84)

READING FROM 'THE SILVER DARLINGS':

"TORMOD GOES FISHING" AN EXTRACT FROM THE CHAPTER
"THE DERELICT BOAT".

17TH MAY 1951

TYPE OF WORK    —    READING

PRODUCER    —    J. GILLESPIE

PROGRAMME    _    SCOTTISH HOME SERVICE-

SCHOOLS PROGRAMME

TIME    —    10 MINUTES

Typescript held at B.B.C. Edinburgh.


E17    (A84)

READING FROM 'THE SILVER DARLINGS'

18TH MAY 1951

TYPE OF WORK    —    READING

PRODUCER    —    J. GILLESPIE

PROGRAMME    —    SCOTTISH HOME SERVICE

SCHOOLS PROGRAMME

TIME    —    10 MINUTES

Typescript held at B.B.C. Edinburgh.


E18                     (A84 A95 E30)

"THIS IS MY COUNTRY" THE HERRING FISHING

NO. 2 'STORM AND PRECIPICE'.

                              28TH    SEPTEMBER    1951

TYPE OF WORK     -     READING FROM 'THE SILVER

                       DARLINGS'

PRODUCER         -     TOM ALLEN

PROGRAMME        -     SCOTTISH HOME SERVICE

                       SCHOOLS PROGRAMME

TIME             -     19 MINUTES

Typescript held at B.B.C. Edinburgh


E19                       (A84)

        "SENIOR ENGLISH II" 'ORDEAL BY PLAGUE'

                              3RD    JUNE    1952

TYPE OF WORK     -     READING FROM 'THE SILVER

                       DARLINGS'

PRODUCER         -     T.S. ALLEN

PROGRAMME        -     SCOTTISH HOME SERVICE

                       SCHOOLS PROGRAMME

TIME             -     19 MINUTES

Typescript held at B.B.C. Edinburgh


E20                     (A123 E48 E66)

        "BOOK BY THE FIRE" - BLOODHUNT

                              12TH   OCTOBER   1952

TYPE OF WORK     -     TALK BY ALAN MELVILLE

PRODUCER         -     NOT KNOWN

PROGRAMME         -    LIGHT PROGRAMME

TIME              -    30 MINUTES

No known typescript or recording held.


E21

"FOR SENIOR SECONDARY SCHOOLS":

'SOME MODERN SCOTTISH WRITERS'.

1ST   JUNE   1953

TYPE OF WORK      -    TALK ABOUT NEIL M. GUNN

                       BY L.A.G. STRONG

PRODUCER          -    GEORGE DIXON

PROGRAMME         -    SCOTTISH HOME SERVICE

                       SCHOOLS PROGRAMME

TIME              -    20 MINUTES

Typescript held at B.B.C. Edinburgh.


E22               (A126)

     "BOOK REVIEW" - THE OTHER LANDSCAPE

2ND   APRIL   1954

TYPE OF WORK      -    REVIEW OF GUNN'S NEW BOOK

                       BY MAURICE LINDSAY

PRODUCER          -    NOT KNOWN

PROGRAMME         -    SCOTTISH HOME SERVICE

TIME              -    15 MINUTES

Typescript held at B.B.C. Edinburgh.


E23               (A92 A94 A95)

   "SENIOR ENGLISH I" 'ART RUNS A GREAT RACE'

11TH   JUNE   1954

TYPE OF WORK      -    READING FROM 'YOUNG ART AND

181

OLD HECTOR'

PRODUCER        -    DAVID BUTTS

PROGRAMME       -    SCOTTISH HOME SERVICE

                     SCHOOLS PROGRAMME

TIME            -    20 MINUTES

Typescript held at B.B.C. Edinburgh.


E24              (A34 A51 A63)

   HERITAGE NO 1 'THE FAMILY FACE' - A PORTRAIT OF

OURSELVES, THE SCOTTISH FAMILY, COMPILED FROM SOME

   SKETCHES BY SOME MEMBERS AND SOME NEIGHBOURS,

          RELATIVES AND VISITORS.

                          19TH  SEPTMEBER  1954

TYPE OF WORK    -    AS ABOVE, CONTAINS EXTRACTS

                     FROM 'THE LOST GLEN' AND

                     'WHISKY AND SCOTLAND'

PRODUCER        -    ROBIN RICHARDSON

PROGRAMME       -    SCOTTISH HOME SERVICE

TIME            -    ONE HOUR

Typescript held at B.B.C. Glasgow (Written by John
Wilson)


E25              (A59 B24 D198)

   HERITAGE NO. 18 'THE HIGHLAND CLEARANCES'

                          12TH  DECEMBER  1954

For details see entry under plays for 12.12.1954.


E26                  (A63)

             HERITAGE NO. 23 'WHISKY'

                          30TH  DECEMBER  1954

For details see entry under plays for 30.12.54.

E27

    HERITAGE NO. 38 'VOICES OF THE NEW SCOTLAND'

                         20TH  MARCH  1955

TYPE OF WORK    -    A REFLECTION WITH ILLUSTRATIONS

                          OF THE MAIN THEMES OF SCOTTISH

                          WRITING DURING THE TWENTIETH

                          CENTURY WITH CONTRIBUTIONS BY

                          NEIL M. GUNN.

PRODUCER      -    ROBIN RICHARDSON

PROGRAMME    -    SCOTTISH HOME SERVICE

TIME        -    ONE HOUR

Typescript held at B.B.C. Glasgow written by John Wilson.


E28

       HERITAGE NO. 39 'REDISCOVERY'

                        24TH  MARCH  1955

TYPE OF WORK    -    AN ACCOUNT OF THE SCOTTISH

                          'RENAISSANCE' MOVEMENT

PRODUCER      -    ROBIN RICHARDSON

PROGRAMME    -    SCOTTISH HOME SERVICE

TIME        -    ONE HOUR

Typescript held at B.B.C. Glasgow.


E29              (A84 E90)

    'THIS IS MY COUNTRY'.  "THE FIRST FISHING"

        FROM THE SILVER DARLINGS

                    14TH  OCTOBER  1955

TYPE OF WORK    -    READING (CHAP.I)

```
PRODUCER          -    TOM ALLEN

PROGRAMME         -    SCOTTISH HOME SERVICE
                       SCHOOLS PROGRAMME

TIME              -    20 MINUTES
```

Typescripts held at B.B.C. Edinburgh and The B.B.C.
Script Library, London.


E30                    (A84 A95 E18)

     "THIS IS MY COUNTRY" 'STORM AND PRECIPICE'

          FROM THE SILVER DARLINGS

                              21ST   OCTOBER   1955

```
TYPE OF WORK      -    READING (CHAP.XV)

PRODUCER          -    TOM ALLEN

PROGRAMME         -    SCOTTISH HOME SERVICE
                       SCHOOLS PROGRAMME

TIME              -    20 MINUTES
```

Typescripts held at B.B.C. Edinburgh and The B.B.C.
Script Library, London.


E31

     "ST. ANDREWS DAY" - LETTERS FROM SCOTLAND

          "FISHING" TO THE REV. R.F.V. SCOTT

                         30TH   NOVEMBER   1955

```
TYPE OF WORK      -    LETTER

PRODUCER          -    ROBIN RICHARDSON

PROGRAMME         -    SCOTTISH HOME SERVICE

TIME              -    3 MINUTES
```

Typescript held at the National Library of Scotland.


E32

"SCOTTISH LIFE AND LETTERS" - 'TIME - A
HIGHLAND REFLECTION'.

8TH   JANUARY   1956

TYPE OF WORK     -     TALK

PRODUCER         -     GEORGE BRUCE

PROGRAMME        -     SCOTTISH HOME SERVICE

TIME             -     9 MINUTES

No known typescript or recording held.


E33          (A96 A112 A130 B21 E9 E10 E71)

WEDNESDAY MATINEE - "SUN AND MOON"

28TH   MARCH   1956

For details see entry under plays 1.6.1944.


E34                    (B26)

THE SEA TO THE ISLES

9TH   AUGUST   1956

For details see entry under plays 9.8.56.


E35

'ANNALS OF SCOTLAND' - "RENAISSANCE?"
(THE SCOTTISH LITERARY REVIVAL THAT FOLLOWED THE
FIRST WORLD WAR)

22ND   NOVEMBER   1956

TYPE OF WORK     -     PERSONAL REMINISCENCE BY NEIL
                       M. GUNN, NARRATED BY ROBERT
                       DUNNETT.

PRODUCER         -     GEORGE BRUCE

PROGRAMME        -     SCOTTISH HOME SERVICE

TIME             -     ONE HOUR.

Typescripts held at B.B.C. Edinburgh and The
National Library of Scotland.


E36      (A24 A33 A34 A40 A107 B5 E4 E11 E58)
   "THE ANNALS OF SCOTLAND" - 'THE DRINKING WELL'
                    3RD DECEMBER 1956
TYPE OF WORK    -    ADAPTION OF NEIL GUNN'S NOVEL
                  BY JOHN WILSON.
PRODUCER       -    FINLAY J. MACDONALD
PROGRAMME      -    SCOTTISH HOME SERVICE
TIME           -    ONE HOUR 30 MINUTES
Typescript held at B.B.C. Glasgow, B.B.C. Script
Library (Plays) London and The National Library of
Scotland.


E37                    (A127)
    "BOOK REVIEW" - THE ATOM OF DELIGHT
               19TH DECEMBER 1956
TYPE OF WORK    -    REVIEW OF NEIL GUNN'S AUTO-
                  BIOGRAPHY BY ROBERT DUNNETT.
PRODUCER       -    NOT KNOWN
PROGRAMME      -    SCOTTISH HOME SERVICE
TIME           -    15 MINUTES
No known typescript or recording held.


E38
"ANNALS OF SCOTLAND" - 'SKETCH BOOK OF THE THIRTIES'
 (AN IMPRESSION BY EDWIN MUIR OF THE LITERATURE OF A
   DECADE OF UNEMPLOYMENT AND APPROACHING WAR)
               20TH JANUARY 1957

TYPE OF WORK       -     CONTAINED EXTRACT FROM 'THE
                         SILVER BOUGH'

PRODUCER       -    ROBIN RICHARDSON

PROGRAMME      -    SCOTTISH HOME SERVICE

TIME           -    50 MINUTES

Typescript held at B.B.C. Script Library (Plays)
London.


E39

       "SCOTTISH LIFE AND LETTERS".

   THE CONTEMPORARY ARTIST AND THE PUBLIC; NO. 12

            THE NOVEL

                              12TH   MARCH   1957

TYPE OF WORK    -    TALK

PRODUCER        -    GEORGE BRUCE

PROGRAMME       -    SCOTTISH HOME SERVICE

TIME            -    10 MINUTES.

Typescript held at The National Library of Scotland.


E40

       "SCOTTISH LIFE AND LETTERS".

    THE CONTEMPORARY ARTIST AND THE PUBLIC;

         NO. 13 THE NOVEL (CONTINUED)

                              26TH   MARCH   1957

TYPE OF WORK    -    TALK

PRODUCER        -    GEORGE BRUCE

PROGRAMME       -    SCOTTISH HOME SERVICE

TIME            -    11 MINUTES

Typescript held at the National Library of Scotland.

E41                    (A127 B27)

THE BOY AND THE SALMON

30TH   MAY   1957

For details see entry under plays 30.5.57.


E42                    (D11 D213 D217)

THE INDIVISIBLE MAN - MEN OF MARK

3RD   JULY   1957

TYPE OF WORK      -    TRIBUTE TO C.M. GRIEVE ON HIS

RECEIVING A DOCTORATE AT

EDINBURGH UNIVERSITY TO WHICH

NEIL GUNN CONTRIBUTED.

PRODUCER          -    ROBIN RICHARDSON

PROGRAMME         -    SCOTTISH HOME SERVICE

TIME              -    45 MINUTES (GUNN'S PART 4M)

No known typescript or recording held although a
typescript at The National Library of Scotland
entitled 'FOR CHRISTOPHERS CAP' probably relates to
this piece.


E43                    (B28)

"THIS IS MY COUNTRY" - LIVING IN THE HIGHLANDS I
'GOOD NEWS COMES TO THE GLEN'

1ST   NOVEMBER   1957

For details see entry under plays 1.11.1957.


E44          (A74 A80 B14 B29 D212)

"THIS IS MY COUNTRY" - LIVING IN THE HIGHLANDS II
'DEER STALKING'

8TH   NOVEMBER   1957

For details see entry under plays 8.11.57.


E45                        (B30)

    "THIS IS MY COUNTRY" - LIVING IN THE HIGHLANDS III

                    'ALL IN A LIFETIME'

                                15TH   NOVEMBER   1957

For details see entry under plays 15.11.57.


E46

                LIFE IN THE HIGHLANDS

                                4TH   MARCH   1958

TYPE OF WORK      -    TALK

PRODUCER          -    BILL MEIKLE

TIME              -    4 MINUTES

Typescript held at National Library of Scotland.


E47

        TIME OUT OF DOORS - ANGLING AND PIGEONS

                                13TH   MARCH   1958

TYPE OF WORK      -    TALK

PRODUCER          -    FRANCIS DILLON

PROGRAMME         -    NETWORK THREE

TIME              -    30 MINUTES

No known typescript or recording held.


E48            (A123 A20 E66)

                    BLOODHUNT

TYPE OF WORK      -    ADAPTION OF NEIL M. GUNN'S

                      NOVEL BY JOHN WILSON

PRODUCER          -    FINLAY J. MACDONALD

                        189

PROGRAMME        -    SCOTTISH HOME SERVICE

TIME             -    ONE HOUR 30 MINUTES

Typescripts held at B.B.C. Glasgow and B.B.C. Script
Library (Plays) London.


E49                          (F17)

  "ARTS REVIEW" - 'THE CHANGELING' BY ROBERT JENKINS

                         30TH   APRIL   1958

TYPE OF WORK     -    BOOK REVIEW

PRODUCER         -    GEORGE BRUCE

PROGRAMME        -    SCOTTISH HOME SERVICE

TIME             -    PROGRAMME 45 MINUTES (GUNN'S

                     CONTRIBUTION 4 MINS)

Typescripts   held   at   B.B.C.   Edinburgh   and   The
National Library of Scotland.


E50

  "SCOTTISH LIFE AND LETTERS" - THE TENTH ANNIVERSARY

                     EDITION

                         14TH   MAY   1958

TYPE OF WORK     -    NEIL GUNN WROTE AND READ THE

                     LINKING NARRATIVE

PRODUCER         -    GEORGE BRUCE

PROGRAMME        -    SCOTTISH HOME SERVICE

TIME             -    45 MINUTES

Typescript held at B.B.C. Edinburgh.


E51                          (A46)

    "THIS IS MY COUNTRY" - "LAND AND SEA"

                         7TH   NOVEMBER   1958

TYPE OF WORK    -    EXTRACTS FROM 'MORNING TIDE'

PRODUCER        -    DAVID BUTTS

PROGRAMME       -    SCOTTISH HOME SERVICE

                     SCHOOLS PROGRAMME

TIME            -    20 MINUTES

Typescript held at B.B.C. Edinburgh


E52                     (A46)

    "SCOTTISH LIFE AND LETTERS" - IS THERE A

    LIVING SCOTTISH TRADITION IN WRITING TODAY?

                              15TH   JANUARY   1959

TYPE OF WORK    -    TALK CONTAINING EXTRACTS

                     FROM MORNING TIDE

PRODUCER        -    GEORGE BRUCE

PROGRAMME       -    SCOTTISH HOME SERVICE

TIME            -    30 MINUTES (GUNN'S CONTRIBUTIO

                     7 MINUTES)

Typescripts held at B.B.C. Glasgow and The National
Library of Scotland.


E53                 (D239 E59 E72)

    "TOWN AND COUNTRY" - 'THE WONDER STORY

        OF THE MORAY FIRTH'

                              28TH   APRIL   1959

TYPE OF WORK    -    TALK

PRODUCER        -    I. GRIMBLE

PROGRAMME       -    SCOTTISH HOME SERVICE ON

                     V.H.F. - LIMITED TRANSMISSION

                     TO MELDRUM AND ROSEMARKIE

                     AREAS

```
TIME            -    15 MINUTES
```

Typescripts held at B.B.C. Glasgow, B.B.C. Script
Library London and The National Library of Scotland.


```
E54                    (A71 D220)
                  THE LIGHT OF IONA
                                        5TH JUNE 1959
TYPE OF WORK     -    TALK
PRODUCER         -    I. GRIMBLE
PROGRAMME        -    THIRD
TIME             -    15 MINUTES
```

Typescript held at B.B.C.  Glasgow, B.B.C.  Script
Library London and The National Library of Scotland.


```
E55                    (E57 E93)
           'SCOTTISH LIFE AND LETTERS' - LANDSCAPE
                                        10TH  JUNE  1959
TYPE OF WORK    -    CONVERSATION
PRODUCER        -    GEORGE BRUCE
PROGRAMME       -    SCOTTISH HOME SERVICE
TIME            -    30 MINUTES
```

Typescripts held at B.B.C.  Glasgow and B.B.C.
Edinburgh.


```
E56
         "ARTS REVIEW" - REVIEW OF 'THE HIGHLANDS'
                  BY CALUM I MACLEAN
                                        24TH  JUNE  1959
TYPE OF WORK     -    BOOK REVIEW
PRODUCER         -    GEORGE BRUCE
```

PROGRAMME          -    SCOTTISH HOME SERVICE

TIME               -    30 MINUTES (GUNN's

                       CONTRIBUTION 3 MINUTES)

Typescripts   held   at   B.B.C.     Edinburgh   and   The
National Library of Scotland.


E57               (A127 E55 E93)

                 TALKING ABOUT LANDSCAPE

                                    28TH   JUNE   1959

TYPE OF WORK      -    CONVERSATION

PRODUCER          -    GEORGE BRUCE

PROGRAMME         -    SCOTTISH HOME SERVICE

TIME              -    15 MINUTES

Typescript held at National Library of Scotland.


E58      (A24 A33 A34 A40 A107 B5 E4 E11 E36)

    'SATURDAY NIGHT THEATRE' - THE DRINKING WELL

                                    18TH   JULY   1959

Recorded repeat of Programme Broadcast 3.12.1956.


E59               (D239 E53 E72)

        THE WONDER STORY OF THE MORAY FIRTH

                                    31ST   JULY   1959

Recorded repeat of Programme Broadcast 28.4.1959.


E60                    (E61)

 "THE WORLD OF BOOKS" - BOOKS WE READ AND READ AGAIN

                                    24TH   OCTOBER   1959

TYPE OF WORK      -    DISCUSSION ON WALTER SCOTT

                       IN WHICH NEIL M. GUNN TOOK

PART

PRODUCER         -    ROBIN HOLMES

PROGRAMME        -    HOME SERVICE LONDON

TIME             -    35 MINUTES

Typescripts held at the B.B.C.   Script Library London and The National Library of Scotland.


E61                    (E60)

"THE WORLD OF BOOKS" - BOOKS WE READ AND READ AGAIN

                           31ST   OCTOBER   1959

Recorded repeat of Programme Broadcast 24.10.1959, put out over Scottish Home Service on this occasion.


E62                    (A84)

'THIS IS MY COUNTRY' - STORIES OF MEN AND THE SEA

                           27TH NOVEMBER 1959

TYPE OF WORK     -    ADAPTATION FROM 'THE SILVER
                     DARLINGS'

PRODUCER         -    TOM ALLEN

PROGRAMME        -    SCOTTISH HOME SERVICE
                     SCHOOLS PROGRAMME

TIME             -    20 MINUTES

Typescript held at B.B.C. Edinburgh.


E63                    (A84)

'THIS IS MY COUNTRY' - STORIES OF MEN AND THE SEA

                           4TH   DECEMBER   1959

TYPE OF WORK     -    ADAPTATION FROM 'THE SILVER
                     DARLINGS'

PRODUCER         -    TOM ALLEN

PROGRAMME        -    SCOTTISH HOME SERVICE

                     SCHOOLS PROGRAMME

TIME             -    20 MINUTES

Typescript held at B.B.C. Edinburgh.


E64                      (E65)

          'TOWN AND COUNTRY' - THE LATE

    MISS MARGARET MACDOUGALL, LIBRARIAN AT INVERNESS

                          26TH   JANUARY   1960

TYPE OF WORK     -    TALK - NARRATOR NEIL M. GUNN

PRODUCER         -    I. GRIMBLE

PROGRAMME        -    SCOTTISH HOME SERVICE ON VHF

                     LIMITED TRANSMISSION TO THE

                     MELDRUM AND ROSEMARKIE AREAS

TIME             -    3 MINUTES

Typescript held at The National Library of Scotland.


E65                      (E64)

          'NORTHERN NOTEBOOK' - THE LATE

    MISS MARGARET MACDOUGALL, LIBRARIAN AT INVERNESS

                          1ST   FEBRUARY   1960

This Programme included a recorded repeat of the
talk given 26.1.1960.


E66                  (A123 E20 E48)

                     BLOODHUNT

                          5TH   MARCH   1960

Recorded repeat of Programme Broadcast 28.4.1958.


E67                      (E68)

'TOWN AND COUNTRY' - THE BEGINNING OF THE PROGRAMME

10TH  MAY  1960

TYPE OF WORK      -    TALK - MAGAZINE PROGRAMME

PRODUCER          -    I. GRIMBLE

PROGRAMME         -    SCOTTISH HOME SERVICE ON VHF

                       LIMITED TRANSMISSION TO

                       MELDRUM, ROSERMARKIE, ORKNEY

                       AND THRUMSTER AREAS.

TIME              -    20 MINUTES (GUNN's

                       CONTRIBUTION 2 MINUTES)

No known typescript or recording held.


E68                      (E67)

'NORTHERN NOTEBOOK' - THE BEGINNING OF THE PROGRAMME

20TH  MAY  1960

This programme included a recorded repeat of the
Broadcast of 10.5.1960.


E69

COUNTERPOINT - TELEVISION BROADCAST WITH

MAURICE LINDSAY

17TH JUNE 1960

TYPE OF WORK      -    FILMED INTERVIEW

PRODUCER          -    GEORGE BRUCE

PROGRAMME         -    TELEVISION - B.B.C. SCOTLAND

TIME              -    30 MINUTES (FILM INSERT

                       15.1/2 MINUTES)

No typescript or recording held but a typescript of
the interview is held at The National Library of
Scotland.

E70

EXPERIENCE INTO NOVEL

19TH JUNE 1960

TYPE OF WORK    -    CONVERSATION (N.M. GUNN AND

MAURICE LINDSAY)

PRODUCER    -    GEORGE BRUCE

PROGRAMME    -    SCOTTISH HOME SERVICE

TIME    -    14 MINUTES

Recording held in the archives of the B.B.C. London.

Typescript held at The National Library of Scotland.


E71    (A96 A112 A130 B21 E9 E10 E33)

SUN AND MOON

29TH JUNE 1960

For details see entry under plays 1.6.1944.


E72    (D239 E53 E59)

'TOWN AND COUNTRY' - THE WONDER STORY OF

THE MORAY FIRTH

9TH AUGUST 1960

Recorded repeat of the Broadcast of 28.4.1959.

Extended also to Orkney and Thrumster Area.


E73

'ARTS REVIEW' - REVIEW OF "A COMMON GRACE"

POEMS BY NORMAN McCAIG

5TH OCTOBER 1960

TYPE OF WORK    -    BOOK REVIEW

PRODUCER    -    GEORGE BRUCE

```
PROGRAMME        -   SCOTTISH HOME SERVICE

TIME             -   25 MINUTES (GUNN's

                     CONTRIBUTION 3 MINUTES)
```

Typescripts held at B.B.C. Edinburgh and The National Library of Scotland.


E74

      'ARTS REVIEW' - REVIEW OF 'THE TROSSACHS

      AND THE ROB ROY COUNTRY' BY CAMPBELL NAIRN

                      21ST   JUNE   1961

```
TYPE OF WORK     -   BOOK REVIEW

PRODUCER         -   GEORGE BRUCE

PROGRAMME        -   SCOTTISH HOME SERVICE

TIME             -   30 MINUTES (GUNN'S

                     CONTRIBUTION 3 MINUTES)
```

Typescripts held at B.B.C. Edinburgh and The National Library of Scotland.


E75

     'ARTS REVIEW' - REVIEW OF 'THE BRAVE WHITE FLAG'

             BY JAMES ALLAN FORD

                    19TH   JULY   1961

```
TYPE OF WORK     -   BOOK REVIEW

PRODUCER         -   GEORGE BRUCE

PROGRAMME        -   SCOTTISH HOME SERVICE

TIME             -   30 MINUTES
```

Typescripts held at B.B.C. Edinburgh and The National Library of Scotland.

E76

'SCOTTISH LIFE AND LETTERS' - TRIBUTE TO
GEORGE BLAKE

27TH SEPTEMBER 1961

TYPE OF WORK    -    TRIBUTE TO WHICH NEIL M. GUNN
                    CONTRIBUTED.

PRODUCER        -    GEORGE BRUCE

PROGRAMME       -    SCOTTISH HOME SERVICE

TIME            -    30 MINUTES

Typescripts held at B.B.C. Edinburgh and The
National Library of Scotland.


E77                    (A107)

WOMAN'S HOUR - 'THE WIFE'

20TH OCTOBER 1961

TYPE OF WORK    -    QUOTES FROM 'THE DRINKING WELL

PRODUCER        -    NOT KNOWN

PROGRAMME       -    LIGHT PROGRAMME

TIME            -    ONE HOUR - (TOTAL)

No known typescript or recording held.


E78                    (E81)

'TOWN AND COUNTRY' - TRIBUTE TO DR. NEIL M. GUNN
(ON THE OCCASION OF HIS 70TH BIRTHDAY ON THE 8TH NOV.)

10TH NOVEMBER 1961

TYPE OF WORK    -    TRIBUTE BY I. GRIMBLE

PRODUCER        -    JAMES WILSON

PROGRAMME       -    SCOTTISH HOME SERVICE ON VHF
                    LIMITED TRANSMISSION TO
                    MELDRUM, ROSERMARKIE,

199

THRUMSTER AND ORKNEY AND

SANDALE AREAS.

TIME            -     15 MINUTES

No known typescript or recording held.


E79              (A84 A102 A127)

    'SCOTTISH LIFE AND LETTERS' 70TH BIRTHDAY

              OF N.M. GUNN

                        18TH  NOVEMBER  1961

TYPE OF WORK    -     QUOTES FROM 1] THE ATOM OF

                     DELIGHT      2]     THE     SILVER

                     DARLINGS   3]  THE  GREEN  ISLE  OF

                     THE GREAT DEEP.

PRODUCER        -     GEORGE BRUCE

PROGRAMME       -     SCOTTISH HOME SERVICE

TIME            -     35 MINUTES

No known typescript or recording held.


E80                    (A68)

              HIGHLAND RIVER

                        12TH  MARCH  1962

TYPE OF WORK    -     ADAPTATION OF GUNN'S NOVEL BY

                     JOHN WILSON

PRODUCER        -     FINLAY J. MACDONALD

PROGRAMME       -     SCOTTISH HOME SERVICE

TIME            -     ONE HOUR 15 MINUTES

Typescript held at the B.B.C. Script Library (Plays)

London.


E81                    (E78)

'NORTHERN NOTEBOOK' - TRIBUTE TO DR. NEIL M. GUNN

12TH MARCH 1962

Recorded repeat of the Broadcast of 10.11.1961


E82

SCOTLAND ON THE SCREEN

1ST APRIL 1962

TYPE OF WORK    -    TALK BY GUNN ON THE MAKING OF

FILMS

PRODUCERS       -    GEORGE BRUCE AND STEWART CONN

PROGRAMME       -    SCOTTISH HOME SERVICE

TIME            -    30 MINUTES

Typescript held at B.B.C. Edinburgh.


E83                    (A84)

THE SILVER DARLINGS

3RD SEPTEMBER 1962

TYPE OF WORK    -    ADAPTATION OF GUNN'S NOVEL BY

JOHN WILSON

PRODUCER        -    FINLAY J. MACDONALD

PROGRAMME       -    SCOTTISH HOME SERVICE

TIME            -    ONE HOUR 30 MINUTES

Typescripts held at B.B.C. Glasgow and B.B.C. Script
Library (Plays) London

An article relating to this Broadcast appeared in the
Radio Times (Scottish Edition) | London | vol 156 |
No. 2025 | P18 | 30.8.1962


E84                    (A84)

PROSE AND VERSE READINGS - NO 12 THE SILVER DARLINGS

THRUMSTER AND ORKNEY AND

SANDALE AREAS.

TIME            -    15 MINUTES

No known typescript or recording held.


E79            (A84 A102 A127)

'SCOTTISH LIFE AND LETTERS' 70TH BIRTHDAY

OF N.M. GUNN

18TH NOVEMBER 1961

TYPE OF WORK    -    QUOTES FROM 1] THE ATOM OF

DELIGHT        2]        THE        SILVER

DARLINGS    3]    THE    GREEN    ISLE    OF

THE GREAT DEEP.

PRODUCER       -    GEORGE BRUCE

PROGRAMME      -    SCOTTISH HOME SERVICE

TIME           -    35 MINUTES

No known typescript or recording held.


E80            (A68)

HIGHLAND RIVER

12TH    MARCH    1962

TYPE OF WORK    -    ADAPTATION OF GUNN'S NOVEL BY

JOHN WILSON

PRODUCER       -    FINLAY J. MACDONALD

PROGRAMME      -    SCOTTISH HOME SERVICE

TIME           -    ONE HOUR 15 MINUTES

Typescript held at the B.B.C. Script Library (Plays)
London.


E81            (E78)

'NORTHERN NOTEBOOK' - TRIBUTE TO DR. NEIL M. GUNN

12TH MARCH 1962

Recorded repeat of the Broadcast of 10.11.1961


E82

SCOTLAND ON THE SCREEN

1ST APRIL 1962

TYPE OF WORK      -    TALK BY GUNN ON THE MAKING OF

FILMS

PRODUCERS         -    GEORGE BRUCE AND STEWART CONN

PROGRAMME         -    SCOTTISH HOME SERVICE

TIME              -    30 MINUTES

Typescript held at B.B.C. Edinburgh.


E83                    (A84)

THE SILVER DARLINGS

3RD SEPTEMBER 1962

TYPE OF WORK      -    ADAPTATION OF GUNN'S NOVEL BY

JOHN WILSON

PRODUCER          -    FINLAY J. MACDONALD

PROGRAMME         -    SCOTTISH HOME SERVICE

TIME              -    ONE HOUR 30 MINUTES

Typescripts held at B.B.C. Glasgow and B.B.C. Script

Library (Plays) London

An article relating to this Broadcast appeared in the

Radio Times (Scottish Edition) | London | vol 156 |

No. 2025 | P18 | 30.8.1962


E84                    (A84)

PROSE AND VERSE READINGS - NO 12 THE SILVER DARLINGS

TYPE OF WORK    -    READINGS FROM THE SILVER
                          DARLINGS

PRODUCER          -    ROBERT GITTINGS

PROGRAMME        -    SCOTTISH HOME SERVICE
                          SCHOOLS PROGRAMME

TIME              -    10 MINUTES

Typescripts held at B.B.C. Script Library London.


E85                 (A68 A95 A100 E80)

                THE SILVER FISH

                PART 1            4TH MARCH 1963

                PART 2            5TH MARCH 1963

                PART 3            6TH MARCH 1963

                PART 4            7TH MARCH 1963

                PART 5            8TH MARCH 1963

TYPE OF WORK    -    AN ADAPTATION OF THE STORY OF
                          KENN AND THE SALMON FROM
                          'HIGHLAND RIVER' READ BY
                          BRYDEN MURDOCH

PRODUCER          -    STEWART CONN

PROGRAMME        -    SCOTTISH HOME SERVICE

TIME              -    8 MINUTES PER PART

Typescript held at B.B.C. Glasgow

An article relating to this Broadcast appeared in the
Radio Times (Scottish Edition) | London | Vol 158 |
No. 2051 | P19 | 28.2.1963


E86                 (A25 A35 A42 A46)

          'THIS IS MY COUNTRY' - NO. 1 FROM THE SEA

TYPE OF WORK      -      ADAPTATION OF SHORT STORY 'THE

                                  SEA'.

PRODUCER          -      NEIL DALGLEISH

PROGRAMME         -      SCOTTISH HOME SERVICE

                                  SCHOOLS PROGRAMME

TIME              -      19 MINUTES

No known typescript or recording held.


E87

                 THE FIRST FORTY YEARS

                             10TH  OCTOBER  1963

TYPE OF WORK      -      TALK BY NEIL M. GUNN ON THE

                                  PHILOSOPHY BEHIND THE NEW

                                  V.H.F PROGRAMME

PRODUCER          -      JAMES WILSON

PROGRAMME         -      45 MINUTES

Typescript held at National Library of Scotland.


E88

                 IN SEARCH OF EDWIN MUIR

                             28TH  APRIL  1964

TYPE OF WORK      -      TALK

PRODUCER          -      MICHAEL BLAKSTAD

PROGRAMME         -      SCOTTISH HOME SERVICE

TIME              -      ONE HOUR

Recording held at B.B.C. London archives, typescript
held at B.B.C. Edinburgh.

There were two further programmes in this series on
the 7th and 13th May 1964 to which Neil Gunn did not

contribute.


E89

'SCOTTISH LIFE AND LETTERS' THE CONTINUING
TRADITION IN SCOTLAND

31ST MAY 1964

TYPE OF WORK      -    TALK

PRODUCER          -    GEORGE BRUCE

PROGRAMME         -    SCOTTISH HOME SERVICE

TIME              -    30 MINUTES

Typescripts held at The National Library of Scotland
and B.B.C. Edinburgh.


E90                    (A84 E29)

'SCOTTISH HERITAGE' - HERRING HARVEST

2) THE FIRST FISHING

11TH  JUNE  1964

TYPE OF WORK      -    EXTRACT FROM 'THE SILVER
                       DARLINGS'.

PRODUCER          -    MARGARET LYFORD-PIKE

PROGRAMME         -    SCOTTISH HOME SERVICE
                       SCHOOLS PROGRAMME

TIME              -    20 MINUTES

Typescript held at B.B.C. Edinburgh.


E91            (A102 E79 E92 E99 E110)

"AFTERNOON THEATRE" THE GREEN ISLE OF THE GREAT DEEP

PART  I          22ND  JANUARY  1966

PART  II         29TH  JANUARY  1966

TYPE OF WORK    -    ADAPTATION OF GUNN'S NOVEL BY

206

JOHN KEIR CROSS

PRODUCER        -    STEWART CONN

PROGRAMME       -    HOME SERVICE AND SCOTTISH

HOME                 SERVICE

TIME            -    ONE HOUR EACH PART

Typescripts held at B.B.C. Script Library (Plays)
London and The National Library of Scotland.

An article relating to the Broadcast appeared in the
Radio Times (Scottish Edition) | London | Vol 170 |
No. 2202 | P9 | 20.1.1966.

Alex MacKenzie who played Old Hector died just before
the broadcast.


E92         (A102 E79 E91 E99 E110)

        THE GREEN ISLE OF THE GREAT DEEP

                    PART I           7TH MAY 1967

                    PART II          14TH MAY 1967

Recorded repeat of the Programmes Broadcast 22.1.1966
and 29.1.1966.


E93              (E55 E57)

        'SCOTTISH LIFE AND LETTERS' LANDSCAPE

     (20 YEARS OF "SCOTTISH LIFE AND LETTERS")

                              25TH MAY 1969

Recorded repeat of Programme Broadcast 10.6.1959.


E94      (A60 A118 A120 A121 D178 E14 E96)

    "AFTERNOON THEATRE" THE WELL AT THE WORLDS END

                    PART I      28TH FEBRUARY 1970

                    PART II       7TH MARCH 1970

                         PART   III              14TH   MARCH   1970

TYPE OF WORK        -    ADAPTATION OF GUNN'S NOVEL BY

                         ALEX REID.

PRODUCER            -    STEWART CONN

PROGRAMME           -    RADIO FOUR

TIME                -    ONE HOUR EACH PART

Typescripts  held  at  B.B.C.  Glasgow,  B.B.C.  Script
Library  (Plays)  London  and  The  National  Library  of
Scotland.

An  article  relating  to  this  Broadcast  Appeared  in  the
Radio  Times  (Scottish  Edition)  |  London  |  Vol  186  |
No.  2416  |  P12  |  26.2.1970


E95

'SCOTTISH LIFE AND LETTERS' A MATTER OF ENLIGHTENMENT

                                       15TH   MARCH   1970

TYPE OF WORK        -    INTERVIEW WITH GEORGE BRUCE

PRODUCER            -    GEORGE BRUCE

PROGRAMME           -    SCOTTISH HOME SERVICE

TIME                -    10 MINUTES

Typescript held at B.B.C. Glasgow.


E96        (A60 A118 A120 A121 D178 E14 E94)

            THE WELL AT THE WORLDS END

                         PART I        26TH SEPTEMBER 1971

                         PART II       19TH SEPTEMBER 1971

                         PART III      26TH SEPTEMBER 1971

Recorded  repeat  of  the  Programmes  Broadcast  28.2.1970
7.3.1970 and 14.3.1970.

E97

THE REALITY AND THE ROMANCE

10TH NOVEMBER 1971

TYPE OF WORK    -    INTERVIEW WITH GEORGE BRUCE

PRODUCER    -    GEORGE BRUCE

PROGRAMME    -    SCOTTISH HOME SERVICE

TIME    -    15 MINUTES

Typescript held at B.B.C. Glasgow.


E98

HIGHLANDS NOVELISTS I

9TH JUNE 1972

TYPE OF WORK    -    PORTRAIT OF NEIL M. GUNN

(UNSCRIPTED INTERVIEW WITH IAN

GRIMBLE - RECORDED 1958)

PRODUCER    -    R.J.C. CRADOCK

PROGRAMME    -    RADIO FOUR

TIME    -    2 MINUTES 55 SECONDS

Typescript held at B.B.C. Script Library London.


E99          (A102 E79 E91 E92 E110)

THE GREEN ISLE OF THE GREAT DEEP

PART I          4TH APRIL 1973

PART II          11TH APRIL 1973

Recorded repeat of Programmes Broadcast 22.1.1966 and
29.1.1966.


E100          (A68)

SCOTTISH WRITING

TYPE OF WORK      -    READING FROM 'HIGHLAND RIVER'

PRODUCER          -    DAVID CAMPBELL

PROGRAMME         -    RADIO SCOTLAND

                  -    SCHOOLS PROGRAMME

TIME              -    20 MINUTES

Typescript held at B.B.C. Edinburgh.


E101                    (A59)

                  SCOTTISH WRITING

                            4TH  OCTOBER  1974

TYPE OF WORK      -    READING FROM 'BUTCHER'S BROOM'

PRODUCER          -    DAVID CAMPBELL

PROGRAMME         -    RADIO SCOTLAND

                  -    SCHOOLS PROGRAMME

TIME              -    20 MINUTES

Typescript held at B.B.C. Edinburgh.


E102                    (A84)

                  SCOTTISH WRITING

                            11TH  OCTOBER  1974

TYPE OF WORK      -    READING FROM 'THE SILVER
                      DARLINGS'

PRODUCER          -    DAVID CAMPBELL

PROGRAMME         -    RADIO SCOTLAND

                      SCHOOLS PROGRAMME

TIME              -    20 MINUTES

Typescript held at B.B.C. Edinburgh.


E103                    (A84)

'SCOTTISH MAGAZINE' - A PEOPLE OF THE SEA

15TH NOVEMBER 1974

TYPE OF WORK      -    READING FROM 'THE SILVER

DARLINGS'

PRODUCER          -    DAVID CAMPBELL

PROGRAMME         -    RADIO SCOTLAND

SCHOOLS PROGRAMME

TIME              -    20 MINUTES

Typescript held at B.B.C. Edinburgh.


E104                    (A84)

'SCOTTISH MAGAZINE' - A PEOPLE OF THE SEA

24TH JANUARY 1976

TYPE OF WORK      -    READING FROM 'THE SILVER

DARLINGS'

PRODUCER          -    DAVID CAMPBELL

PROGRAMME         -    RADIO SCOTLAND

SCHOOLS PROGRAMME

TIME              -    20 MINUTES

Typescript held at B.B.C. Edinburgh.


E105

NEIL M. GUNN - THE MAN AND THE WRITER

2ND MAY 1976

TYPE OF WORK      -    AN APPRECIATION BY IAN GRIMBLE

NARRATED BY TOM FLEMING AND

CONTAINING EXTRACTS FROM

PREVIOUS BROADCASTS.

PRODUCER          -    FRASER STEEL

PROGRAMME         -    RADIO THREE (MANCHESTER)

```
TIME               -   45 MINUTES
```

No known typescript or recording held.

```
E106                    (A84)
```

    'SCOTTISH MAGAZINE' - A PEOPLE OF THE SEA I

                             10TH JANUARY 1978

```
TYPE OF WORK    -   READING FROM 'THE SILVER
                   DARLINGS'
PRODUCER        -   DAVID CAMPBELL
PROGRAMME       -   RADIO SCOTLAND
                   SCHOOLS PROGRAMME
TIME            -   20 MINUTES
```

Typescript held at B.B.C. Edinburgh.

Extract printed in B.B.C. Radio Teachers Notes Spring/Summer 1978 PP3-4.

```
E107                    (A84)
```

    'SCOTTISH MAGAZINE' - A PEOPLE OF THE SEA II

                             17TH JANUARY 1978

```
TYPE OF WORK    -   READING FROM 'THE SILVER
                   DARLINGS'
PRODUCER        -   DAVID CAMPBELL
PROGRAMME       -   RADIO SCOTLAND
                   SCHOOLS PROGRAMME
TIME            -   20 MINUTES
```

Typescript held at B.B.C. Edinburgh.

Extract printed in B.B.C. Radio Teachers Notes Spring/Summer 1978 PP3-4.

```
E108                    (A84,E109)
```

THE SILVER DARLINGS

|          |                 |
|----------|-----------------|
| PART I   | 13TH JUNE 1982  |
| PART II  | 20TH JUNE 1982  |
| PART III | 27TH JUNE 1982  |
| PART IV  | 4TH JULY 1982   |
| PART V   | 11TH JULY 1982  |

TYPE OF WORK    -    ADAPTATION OF GUNN'S NOVEL BY

TOM McGRATH.

PRODUCER    -    TOM KINNINMONT

PROGRAMME    -    RADIO 4

TIME    -    ONE HOUR EACH PART


E109                        (A84 E108)

THE SILVER DARLINGS

|          |                 |
|----------|-----------------|
| PART I   | 16TH JUNE 1982  |
| PART II  | 22ND JUNE 1982  |
| PART III | 29TH JUNE 1982  |
| PART IV  | 6TH JULY 1982   |
| PART V   | 13TH JULY 1982  |

Recorded repeat of the programmes broadcast 13.6.1982, 20.6.1982, 27.6.1982, 4.7.1982 and 11.7.1982.


The recording of the first part was scheduled for 15th June 1982 and appeared as such in "The Radio Times". It was deferred to allow for coverage of the Falklands war.


E110          (A102 E79 E91 E92 E99)

THE GREEN ISLE OF THE GREAT DEEP

PART I          4TH JANUARY 1986

213

Recorded repeat of programmes Broadcast 22.1.1966 and 29.1.1966.

F

MISCELLANEOUS

F1                    (A1 C1)

Vol I   No I   MAY 1918 of THE APPLE TREE contained
extracts of GUNN'S entries for various competitions
organised by and for Members of the Aspirants
Fellowship.


F2

Contribution to 'LETTERS TO THE EDITOR | THE   GLASGOW
HERALD | GLASGOW.

                    P11        26TH NOVEMBER 1928

Written under the pseudonym of Dane McNeil.


F3

        SCOTS POETRY | INVERNESS COURIER | INVERNESS
ISSUE NO. 8639   P3   COL.B.

                                        24TH MAY 1929

Article appears over the initials N.M.G.
Review of:-

        THE SINGIN' LASS      -      MARION ANGUS

        IN QUIET FIELDS       -      ROBERT CRAWFORD


F4

        LETTER | JOHN O'GROAT JOURNAL | WICK
VOL 93   NO 4831   P.6   COL 4

                                        7TH JUNE 1929

Letter relates to Hugh MacDiarmid, and also comments
on a poem by Arthur Ball.
Primarily the Letter responds to criticism of GUNN'S
Article in the Wick Mercantile Debating Society
Magazine of April 1929.

F5

    LETTER | THE SCOTS INDEPENDENT | GLASGOW
VOL 5 NO 6 P 94

                                        APRIL  1931
Written under the pseudonym of Dane McNeil


F6

LETTER CONTRIBUTED TO:-

     'SCOTLAND  IN  QUEST  OF  HER  YOUTH'  EDITED  BY
     D.C.  THOMPSON | OLIVER & BOYD | EDINBURGH
PP 163 - 164                                1932
From  a  date  on  the  introduction  the  date  of
publication would seem to have been August.


F7

REVIEW OF 'SCOTT AND SCOTLAND' BY EDWIN MUIR | THE
              SCOTS MAGAZINE | DUNDEE
VOL 26  NO 1  PP 72 - 78              OCTOBER 1936


F8

REVIEW OF "A HANDFUL OF EARTH" BY WM. SOUTER | OUTLOOK
                  | EDINBURGH
VOL 1  NO 9  PAGE 80              DECEMBER 1936


F9

     FOREWORD TO 'THE SCOTTISH FISHERIES -
              ARE THEY DOOMED'
              BY PETER F. ANSON
PUBLISHED FOR THE BELHAVEN PRESS BY OLIVER AND BOYD |
EDINBURGH | 1939

PP 3 - 7

F10

CONTRIBUTION TO 'LETTERS TO THE EDITOR' | THE GLASGOW
                      HERALD | GLASGOW
P 2                                    6TH JUNE 1942


F11

FOREWORD TO 'THE CULTURE OF THE SCOT' ITS PAST AND
FUTURE BY WILLIAM POWER
PUBLISHED   FOR   SCOTTISH   CONVENTION   BY   WILLIAM
MACLELLAN, 240 HOPE STREET, GLASGOW
PP 5 - 7                                        1943


F12

BOOKS AND OTHER THINGS - A REVIEW | THE SCOTS
                    MAGAZINE | DUNDEE
VOL 41   NO 2   PP 162 - 164              MAY 1944


F13

    SPEECH GIVEN ON THE OCCASION OF RECEIVING HIS
    HONORARY DEGREE (LLD) AT EDINBURGH UNIVERSITY
                          2ND  JULY  1948
Typescript held at the National Library of Scotland.


F14

INTRODUCTION TO THE PROGRAMME FOR 'HERTFORDSHIRE
                    HIGHLAND GAMES'
PAGE 3                              13TH JUNE 1953
Gathering  (The  Fifth)  held  at  Rothamsted  Park,

Harpenden

Chieftan Lt.Col. D.H. Cameron of Lochiel, T.D.

26th Chief of Clan Cameron.


F15

SURVEYING IN THE HIGHLANDS — CAN THE CROFTS BE

REVIVED | THE MANCHESTER GUARDIAN | MANCHESTER

NO 33834    PAGE 6    COL F - G                    7.4.1955

Review of a book by Fraser Darling.


F16                        (A127)

   LETTER RE: 'THE ATOM OF DELIGHT' | THE CAMBRIDGE

                     REVIEW | CAMBRIDGE

VOL 78   NO 1905   P 522                27TH APRIL 1957


F17                        (E49)

         ARTS REVIEW | SCOTTISH FIELD | GLASGOW

VOL 105   NO 666   P 56                       JUNE 1958

Review of "The Changeling" by Robert Jenkins — From

the B.B.C. Review of 30.4.58

Typescript held at the National Library of Scotland.


F18

FOREWORD TO 'A CROFT IN THE HILLS' BY KATHERINE

STEWART

Published by:-

OLIVER & BOYD LTD | EDINBURGH | 1960 PPix-x

COUNTRY BOOK CLUB EDITION | LONDON | 1961 PPix-x

CLUB LEABHAR LTD | INVERNESS | 1971              PP(ix-x)

Un-numbered

MELVEN PRESS | PERTH | 1979 (INTRODUCTION)

Typescript held with miscellaneous papers at The National Library of Scotland.


F19

## SPEECH WRITTEN FOR THE OPENING OF THE UNIVERSITY GRANTS COMMITTEE CONFERENCE

MAY 1964

Typescript held at the National Library of Scotland.


F20

### PORTRAIT

OCTOBER 1965

Typescript of an address given by GUNN to the Caithness C. C. on being presented with a portrait, painted by D. M. Sutherland.


F21  COMMENTS ON 'LITERATURE NOW' AN ARTICLE BY

G.S.FRASER | POINT | LEICESTER

NO 3   PAGE 56                          SUMMER 1968

The article appeared in the same issue.


F22

COMMENTS ON 'AS SIMPLE AS POSSIBLE' AN ARTICLE BY

J.B. PICK | POINT | LEICESTER

NO 3   PAGE 24                          SUMMER 1968

The article appeared in the same issue.


F23

FOREWORD TO 'LIFE ON LOW SHORE' BY PETER F. ANSON

PUBLISHED BY BANFFSHIRE JOURNAL | BANFF | 1969

PP 11 - 12

Typescript held at the National Library of Scotland.


F24

FOREWORD TO 'THE CAITHNESS BOOK' ED. DONALD OMAND

PUBLISHED BY HIGHLAND PRINTERS LTD | INVERNESS

PP xiii - xiv                                        1972


F25

SALMON FISHING

Typescript of an interview given by GUNN on the above subject is held at the National Library of Scotland. Date and occassion not known.


F26

ADDRESS GIVEN BY GUNN ON SCOTLAND

Typescript held at the National Library of Scotland - No Date.


F27

SCOTTISH LITERATURE

Typescript of an interview given by GUNN on the above subject is held at the National Library of Scotland. Date and occassion not known.


F28

ADDRESS GIVEN BY GUNN ON THE SCOTTISH TRADITION

Typescript held at the National Library of Scotland.

F29

THE UNDERMENTIONED MANUSCRIPT NOTES AND NOTEBOOKS
ARE ON DEPOSIT WITH THE NATIONAL LIBRARY OF
SCOTLAND.

1) 7 Notebooks containing Drafts of Letters,
   Articles and Addresses 1953 - 1970

2) Notebook comprising a diary for July - Sept.
   1939 with comments on current events.

3) Notebook comprising (at one end) a Diary for
   October 21st - 27th, and (at other end) notes
   and quotations from books read.

4) Notebook containing (at one end) notes on the
   British Herring Fishing Company, Gaelic proverbs
   and a Bibliography of the North-East Coast, and
   (at the other end) notes and quotations from
   books read.

5) Five notebooks containing notes and quotations
   from books read.

6) Notebook containing notes on the Gaelic Language
   and Passages in Gaelic.

7) Notebook containing notes on the Isle of Eigg,
   Lismore, Iona, St. Columba and also on Geology.

8) Notebook containing notes on the History of
   Whisky Distilling.

9) Two notebooks 1939 containing corrected
   manuscript drafts of "TO THE WEST", "ACROSS THE
   MINCH", "IN STORNOWAY", "ON BERNERA" and "TO THE
   FLANNAN ISLES"

10) Address Book

11) Notes and Leaflets relating to a journey in

Denmark.

12) Two notebooks, one 1937, containing manuscript notes and drafts for "OFF IN A BOAT", and the other containing excerpts from the Log Book of the "MAGGIE" of Wick (1873)

F30

Various correspondence files both with publishers and personal are held at the National Library of Scotland.

G

INDEX

| | |
|---|---|
| LOST CHART (THE) | A112 |
| LOST GLEN (THE) | A34 A51 |
| LOST WOMAN (THE) | A117 |
| LOVE'S DIALECTIC | A85 |
| | |
| MACDOUGALL, THE LATE MISS MARGARET, LIBRARIAN AT INVERNESS | E64 E65 |
| MACGILLIVRAY - SOURCES OF HIS GENIUS | D28 |
| MAJORCA : IDEA FOR A FILM | B35 |
| MAKING A ROCK GARDEN | D103 |
| MALT WHISKIES | D218 |
| MAN'S LIFE (A) | D91 |
| MAN WHO CAME BACK (THE) | A33 |
| MARCH AND THE DEAD EARTH | D79 |
| MATTER OF ENLIGHTENMENT (A) | E95 |
| MERRIE MONTH OF MAY (THE) | D84 |
| MIDSUMMER OF FOXES AND WILD CATS | D109 |
| MIRACULOUS (THE) | D241 |
| MIRROR (THE) | A38 |
| MOLE CATCHER (THE) | D108 |
| MONTH IN SCOTLAND (THE) | D164 |
| MONTROSE RIDES BY | A66 |
| MOOR (THE) | A37 |
| MORAL OF THE MIDGE (THE) | D156 |
| MORE FISHING LOCHS - AND A FEAST | D143 |
| MORNING TIDE | A46 |
| MUSICAL DOORS | A28 |
| MY BEST DAYS FISHING | D10 |
| MY BIT OF BRITAIN | D115 |
| MYTH OF THE CANNY SCOT (THE) | D253 |

MYTH OF THE GLOOMY SCOT (THE)            D254